What Were the Crusades?

What Were the Crusades?

Third Edition

JONATHAN RILEY-SMITH

IGNATIUS PRESS
San Francisco

First edition 1977
Second edition 1992
Third edition 2002
Published by
IGNATIUS PRESS
San Francisco
and
PALGRAVE MACMILLAN
Basingstoke, England and New York

This book is printed on paper suitable for recycling and made from fully managed and sustained forest sources.

ISBN 0–89870–954–7
Library of Congress Control Number 2002109746

Printed and bound in Great Britain by
J. W. Arrowsmith, Bristol

In memoriam

John James Craik Henderson, 1890–1971

Contents

Contents

Preface

In this book I have put down thoughts that have developed in over a decade of lecturing to and supervising students at the universities of St Andrews and Cambridge, so my first expression of thanks must be to them, especially Dr Bruce Beebe, whose unpublished thesis on King Edward I of England and the crusades is a good study of an aspect of the movement in the late thirteenth century. I am glad to have the chance of stating again how much I appreciate the wise advice of Dr R. C. Smail, my *magister*, who read the book in typescript, as did my wife, whose reactions as a 'general reader' have been of great value to me. I am, as always, grateful to her and to my children for providing the kind of environment in which I find it easy to work.

Cambridge   J. S. C. R.-S.

Preface to Second Edition

The first edition of this book led to quite a fierce debate on the nature of crusading. Most historians now appear to agree that crusades in theatres of war other than the East were regarded by men and women of the time as equally valid expressions of the movement; and new studies of the movement in Spain, the Baltic region and Italy, and of the twelfth- and thirteenth-century critics have contributed to this growing consensus.

But in fact, few fields of history have been subjected to such rapid changes in recent years. Scholars have been turning away from the idea that the majority of crusaders were materialistic in motivation. The image of the landless younger son riding off in search of land and wealth has been replaced by a more complex picture of nobles and knights – very little is known about the peasants – making sacrifices which affected not only themselves but also their families. In consequence, an interest in the religious and social ideas of the laity as a background to motivation is growing. Thought has also been given to the indulgence, although more work is required before its development becomes entirely clear. And there have been major studies of individual expeditions, together with particularly important research on crusading in the fourteenth, fifteenth and sixteenth centuries. It is now clear that the fourteenth century, like the thirteenth, was one in which there was hardly a year in which a crusade was not being waged somewhere.

I have tried to incorporate the new discoveries and perceptions into this edition, while retaining the original thrust of argument: that the starting-point for any study of the crusades must be what the Church, their justifier and authorizer, thought of them.

Windsor   J. S. C. R.-S.

Preface to Third Edition

Nearly 40 years ago Professor Hans Mayer drew attention to all the research that was going on into the crusades without there being any commonly agreed starting-point and appealed for 'an unambiguous, lucid and generally accepted definition of the term "crusade"'. In writing this little book I had the aim of defining it as simply as possible in the hope it would prove useful as something to which students could turn before they read the more ambitious histories. I also wanted to stimulate some discussion of first principles and in that I certainly succeeded, although with results that were not always comfortable. Professor Giles Constable has recently categorized the various schools of thought on definition as:

the **generalists**, who believe that any attempt is more limiting than helpful and hold that any Christian religious war fought for God, or in the belief that its prosecution was furthering his intentions for mankind, was a crusade. Close to them, in my opinion, is the idiosyncratic approach of one recent historian, who, in rejecting definition, argues that it is modern scholars who have given form to − his word is 'invented' − concepts and structures which were in fact being remanufactured to suit the Church and the upper echelons of society at different times and cannot be said to have had any independent existence;

the **popularists**, who propose that the essence of crusading lay in a prophetic, eschatalogical, collective exaltation arising in the peasantry and the urban proletariat;

the **traditionalists**, who treat as authentic only the expeditions launched for the recovery of Jerusalem or in its defence; and the **pluralists**, who maintain that an array of campaigns, preached as crusades and fought by men and women who had taken crusade vows and enjoyed crusade privileges, were as authentic as those to or in aid of Jerusalem, although many of them took place in other theatres of war.

Constable has pointed out that 'the traditionalists ask where a crusade was going... The pluralists, on the other hand, ask how a crusade was initiated and organized'. The definition I give in this book is a pluralist one. Like any model, it is not entirely satisfactory, but it has proved to be hard to come up with anything better, which is why most crusade historians now hold to it. New developments, moreover, appear to confirm its validity. Research on sermons, which is one of the growth areas in modern crusade studies, has revealed more evidence for the use of similar language in different theatres of war. And work on liturgy is finding much the same thing. My argument, therefore, stands, although I have tried to take account of the new research which is enlarging our vision year by year. In particular, I have become much more aware of the penitential element in crusading and the way it coloured the whole movement. I now believe that it was its most important defining feature.

In a research career of over 40 years I have tried to understand crusaders and the ideas they expressed, recognizing that we can never penetrate deeply into the minds of men and women in the past. I have accepted the crusaders for what they were and I have refused to be judgemental. I have approached them in the way, I like to think, an anthropologist might study a people with different ethics and priorities to his own. Like others in my subject, however, I am researching a movement and a body of ideas which are discredited and I have to face the fact that the crusades are nowadays seen through lenses distorted by attitudes to them which evolved in the nineteenth century. A sign that crusading had really come to an end was its romanticization by artists like Sir Walter Scott and Giuseppe Verdi. There was also the moral repugnance felt by liberal thinkers, tinged in northern Europe and

America by Protestant disapproval of what were considered to be typical manifestations of Catholic bigotry and zealotry. And towards the end of the age of positive imperialism crusading was secularized, stripped of its ethos and explained in social and economic terms as proto-colonialism. These attitudes, leading to images of crusades and crusaders which were caricatures, are still with us, deforming academic as well as popular history. I have always believed that objectivity and empathy demand that we abandon them, because otherwise we will never understand a movement which touched the lives of the ancestors of everyone of European descent.

Cambridge   J. S. C. R.-S.

1 *What Were the Crusades?*

The crusading movement was one of the great forces in our history. Fought on a vast scale, in terms of geography and the numbers of men and women involved, the crusades dominated the thoughts and feelings of western Europeans between 1095 and 1500 so profoundly that there was scarcely a writer on contemporary affairs who did not at some point refer to one of them or to the fate of the settlements established in their wake on the eastern shores of the Mediterranean, in Spain and along the Baltic coast. They still had some appeal as late as the eighteenth century. Even today it is hard to be indifferent to their history: they were launched in support of a cause which has been portrayed as the most noble and the most ignoble, and over the centuries men have turned to them for inspiration or as an object lesson in human corruptibility. In modern times the French have seen them as the first of their nation's colonial enterprises. In Palestine the British in 1917 and the Israelis since the 1940s have felt themselves to be the inheritors of their traditions. In the 1960s a movement in the Christian churches, consisting of theologians of Liberation and activists of the new Left, expressed, without seeming to realize the fact, some of the ideas of the crusade theoreticians; so, equally unconscious of the precedents, do modern apologists for 'humanitarian' warfare. For good or ill, the crusades introduced new forces into the politics of the eastern Mediterranean region which were to last for over 600 years and they helped to foster elements in Latin Christianity which are now seen as integral to it.

Yet, the fact that after nearly a millennium of interest and centuries of academic study many people still have no clear idea of what a crusade was demonstrates that definition is not easy. One cannot help wondering how to avoid gross oversimplification when trying to describe something which dominated Europe for so long. The movement took a century to achieve coherence and thereafter it adapted to circumstances. Not all crusades were the large, elaborately organized affairs which have rather inaccurately been given numbers by historians. They could be very small or made up of scattered bands of men departing at different times over several years: in certain periods – the 1170s or the later thirteenth century – much crusading took this form. There was no one term consistently used to describe a crusade or its participants. Besides the various vernacular words which appeared in the thirteenth century, like *croiserie* in French and English, a crusade could be called a pilgrimage (*iter* or *peregrinatio*), a holy war (*bellum sacrum* or *guerre sainte*), a passage or general passage (*passagium generale*), an expedition of the Cross (*expeditio crucis*) or the business of Jesus Christ (*negotium Jhesu Christi*): it is worth noticing how many of these terms were euphemisms. From the first crusaders were referred to as *crucesignati*, 'signed with the Cross', but for centuries they were also called pilgrims, especially, but not exclusively, if they were campaigning to the East. The problem was, of course, that crusading became such a familiar element in the medieval landscape that it did not need to be described in detail.

Contemporaries knew perfectly well what a crusade was. How did they recognize one? In the writings of chroniclers, apologists and canon lawyers, and in the wording of the phrases used by those who drew up papal general letters, we can identify the signs that informed the faithful that a crusade was being preached. First, the participants, or some of them, were called upon to take the Cross, which is to say that they were to make a vow to join a military expedition with defined aims. At that moment each of them was required to attach a cloth cross to his or her clothing and was expected to wear that distinctive emblem continuously until the vow had been fulfilled. The vow they took was of a special kind, and I shall have something to say about it later, but for the moment what is relevant is that in a formal, public ceremony men and women, rich and poor, priests and laymen, made a voluntary promise to take part in the campaign and could be identified as having done so.

We must, however, never think of a crusade as containing only crusaders, for their numbers, especially in the later expeditions, were often quite small: there were always many hangers-on and camp followers attached to an army, while it became common for large numbers of professional soldiers to be employed and even for crusaders to travel East with sums of money with which to buy mercenaries. A common practice, which was associated with crusading but did not involve taking the Cross, was for knights, known as *milites ad terminum*, to commit themselves as an act of devotion to service in the Holy Land or with one of the military orders for a fixed term. By the thirteenth century, moreover, many who took the Cross never actually departed on campaign. Taking advantage of what was known as substitution or redemption, which I will describe later, they sent another in their place or contributed sums of money instead of going, thus helping to finance an expedition.

The second sign that a crusade was being prepared was that those taking the Cross were answering a call that could only be made by the pope in his capacity as Christ's vicar or representative. Thirdly, in consequence of their vows and the performance of the actions promised, the crusaders gained certain well-known privileges. These were subject to development and new rights were added to those originally granted, but we may say that all crusaders were assured that their families, interests and assets would be protected in their absence.

Fourthly, they enjoyed indulgences. The indulgence, which I will describe later, expressed the fact that the most characteristic feature of crusading was that it was penitential. Crusaders had engaged themselves to fight as an act of penance in which they repaid God what was due to him on account of their sins. An indulgence could only be granted by the pope or his agents and it was references to it in papal letters that really informed people that a crusade was being promoted.

A striking feature of the indulgences, or in the case of early crusades the 'remissions of sins', granted to the participants in some military campaigns that took place in Western and Central Europe was that they were specifically associated with those given to crusaders going to recover Jerusalem or defend the Holy Land.

> We concede to all fighting firmly in this expedition the same remission of sins which we have given to the defenders of the Eastern Church. (Pope Calixtus II in 1123 concerning Spain)

> To all those who do not receive the same Cross of Jerusalem and determine to go against the Slavs and remain in that expedition we concede ... that remission of sins which our predecessor Pope Urban of happy memory instituted for those going to Jerusalem. (Pope Eugenius III in 1147 concerning Germany)

> We grant the indulgence ... to all those who undertake this labour personally or at their expense and to those who do not personally take part but send suitable warriors at their own expense, according to their means and quality, and also to those who personally assume this burden at another's expense, and we wish them to enjoy that privilege and immunity which were conceded in the general council to those aiding the Holy Land. (Pope Innocent IV in 1246, proclaiming war against Emperor Frederick II)

> We have thought it worthy to concede those indulgences which in similar cases were accustomed to be given by the Holy See to those going to the aid of the Holy Land. (Pope John XXII in 1326, concerning Spain)

Reading these and other grants of the indulgence, it is clear that to the papal *Curia* many of the expeditions in Spain, along the shores of the Baltic, against heretics and schismatics and even against secular powers in Western Europe were to be regarded as belonging to the same species as crusades to the East, although it should be stressed that the absence of a reference to the Holy Land in a papal general letter is not certain evidence that no equation with the crusades to Palestine was assumed: the Livonian Crusade of 1199 was certainly associated in the minds of contemporaries with those in the East, even though this was not made clear in the surviving authorization of Pope Innocent III. Expressions of the same attitude can be found in liturgies, in the writings of canon lawyers, in the sermons of preachers and in the thirteenth-century practice of commutation, by which a man could change the terms of a vow made, say, to help the Holy Land into participation in a European campaign. The popes who granted indulgences for volunteers fighting in these other theatres of war seem to have believed that crusading was too useful an instrument to be confined to expeditions destined for Jerusalem or sent to the aid of Christian Palestine, even if the Eastern crusades provided the measure against which all others were judged. And in so far as they responded to the appeals and fought in campaigns in Spain and the Baltic region and elsewhere, the volunteers demonstrated that they shared the opinion of the popes.

To contemporaries a crusade was an expedition authorized by the pope on Christ's behalf, the leading participants in which took vows and consequently enjoyed the privileges of protection at home and the indulgence, which, when the campaign was not destined for the East, was equated with that granted to crusaders to the Holy Land. This enables us to identify what was regarded as a crusade, but it cannot take us much further. We can only find out what qualified an expedition for papal authorization of this particular kind by examining the features common to those we have recognized as crusades. Even though the expeditions to the East, and many of those in the West as well, were treated as pilgrimages, they were, of course, wars as well and a useful approach is to look at them against the background of Christian ideas on the use of force.

5

If there are occasions on which war is justifiable, and at least since the fourth century many have believed that there are such occasions, we must admit that in certain circumstances the Fifth Commandment, enshrining a divine prohibition against homicide, can be set aside. But what are those circumstances? There have been two distinct answers to this question provided by those Christians who are not pacifists. The first, which is the most commonly held today and is, curiously, the only one discussed at length by modern moral theologians, is usually called the Theory of the Just War. Its premise is that violence is an evil, but it recognizes that, in intolerable conditions and provided that it is subject to stringent rules, war may be condoned by God as the lesser of evils, although any positive aspect to it is limited to the aims of the restoration of order or the status quo. Around AD 400 St Augustine of Hippo, the first and still the most sophisticated Christian thinker on violence, tried to define the criteria to which war must accord before it could be considered to be justifiable. These were later reduced, and greatly simplified, by theologians and canon lawyers to three. First, the war must have a *just cause* and normally such a cause could only be past or present aggression or injurious action by another. Secondly, it must rest on what was known as the *authority of the prince*. In other words, it must be proclaimed by a legitimate authority, usually, of course, secular, although we will see that it was a churchman with powers encompassing the authorization of war who proclaimed a crusade. Five centuries before the crusades these first two criteria had been summed up by Isidore of Seville in a sentence which passed into the collections of canon law: 'That war is lawful and just which is waged upon command in order to recover property or to repel attack.' The third criterion was known as *right intention*. Each of the participants ought to have pure motives and war must be the only apparently practicable means of achieving the justifiable purpose for which it was to be fought; even then, no more force ought to be used than was strictly necessary.

Just War theory in its present form has inherited these criteria, but has synthesized them with other principles, including the conviction that violence is intrinsically evil, which it seems to have borrowed from pacifism in the first half of the nineteenth century. Before 1800, however, another justification for setting aside the Fifth Commandment prevailed, generated by a much more positive attitude to the use of force. It was generally agreed that violence was not intrinsically evil, but was morally neutral and drew moral colouring from the intentions of the perpetrators. It was, therefore, theoretically possible to envisage 'good' violence and even 'just' persecution. This provided one of the foundations of the medieval concept of Holy War. Another was the conviction that God was intimately associated with a political structure or course of political events in this world which was the product of his will. So violence in support of that polity or course of events was believed to advance his intentions for mankind. It still had to be justified as a necessary but unpleasant reaction to injustice or aggression, but it was also a positive step in accordance with God's wishes. Holy wars could only be waged, as the theologian Jacques Maritain recognized 60 years ago, when the temporal order and God's intentions became inextricably bound up with one another.

A crusade, however, was a special kind of holy war in that it was also penitential. It was at first associated with pilgrimage to Jerusalem, the most penitential goal of all, and a place where devout Christians went to die, which may be why so many of the earliest crusaders were old men. The Cross was invariably enjoined on men and women not as a service, but as a penance, the association of which with war had first been made about a decade before the preaching of the First Crusade. I will consider this in more detail later, but it is important to recognize that crusaders believed they were embarking on a campaign in which their obligations, at any rate if completed, would constitute for each of them an act of condign self-punishment. They were not supposed to travel gloriously, but to dress simply as pilgrims with their arms and armour carried in sacks on pack animals. In 1099, after the fall of Jerusalem, many of the survivors of the campaign threw away their arms and armour and returned to Europe carrying only the palm fronds they had collected as evidence that they had completed their pilgrimage. One of them, Rotrou of Perche, the count of Mortagne, deposited his palms on the altar of his family's foundation, the abbey of Nogent-le-Rotrou.

The conviction that it was holy and penitential did not exempt a crusade from adherence to the principles underlying, and to a certain extent limiting, the bearing of arms by Christians; indeed the belief that it was also penitential reinforced them. In particular, it had to conform to the criteria of the just cause, the authority of the prince and right intention. Of course it would be absurd to suppose that all crusades had causes that reputable theologians would consider to be just or that all crusaders had pure motives, but aberrations do not invalidate what a crusade ought to have been, although studies of them certainly cast light on the practical application of the crusading ideal. Apologists were careful to write of the indulgence being enjoyed only by those whose motives could not be impugned, and went to great lengths to show how campaigns were justly caused – important because the crusaders were volunteers and, like most men and women, would not generally take part in something obviously unjustifiable. This book is concerned with definition, not with judgements on the motives of individual crusaders or the worth of individual campaigns.

2 *A Just Cause*

A Just Cause for War

By the middle of the thirteenth century Christian writers were generally in agreement that the just cause for a war must be reactive and their views prevail today. It is just to defend one's country, laws and traditional way of life, just to try to recover property unlawfully taken by another, perhaps even just to enforce by physical means a properly delivered judicial sentence. It is not just to wage a war of aggrandizement or conversion. This principle applied to the crusade no less than to any other war, but in the first century of the movement other justifications were also being put forward. St Augustine's definition of just violence, that it avenged injuries, presupposed a less passive attitude on the part of the just than was later to be acceptable, especially in the notion of vengeance, which haunted canon lawyers until *c.*1200, after which it seems gradually to have been dropped, and in a wide interpretation of the injuries to be avenged, which could include any violation of righteousness, God's laws or Christian doctrine. As late as the middle of the thirteenth century the great canon lawyer Hostiensis (d. 1271) seems to have believed that Christendom had an intrinsic right to extend its sovereignty over any society which did not recognize the rule of the Roman Church or Roman Empire.

There always seems to have been confusion whether or not a crusade could be waged as a war of conversion and at the time of the First Crusade some came perilously near to promoting it as such. The author of one narrative account, Robert the Monk (or of Rheims), made Pope Urban II at Clermont remind his audience of Charlemagne and Louis the Pious and other Frankish kings 'who destroyed the kingdoms of the pagans and incorporated them within the boundaries of Holy Church'. And in a letter sent to the pope in 1098, after they had taken Antioch in Syria, the leaders of the crusade wrote that they had fought against Turks and pagans but not against heretics and begged Urban to come himself to eradicate all heresies. The waging of a missionary war against the heathen, which had long been an element in German thought, was a prominent theme in 1147, during the preparations for a crusade against the pagans in north-eastern Europe. The papal letter *Divina dispensatione*, which authorized this German expedition, emphasized conversions, in this echoing St Bernard, responsible above all for the pope's support, who in his letters forbade any truce with the pagans 'until such time as, with God's help, they shall be either converted or wiped out'.

It should be stressed that nowhere in *Divina dispensatione* did Pope Eugenius III explicitly justify the crusade as a war of conversion and that St Bernard's approach was not as simple as the quotation given above would suggest: to him the pagans directly threatened Christendom and it was only because there was no alternative to the use of physical force that they must be crushed if they would not be converted. But missions and war were always closely associated in the northern crusades and it was in connection with one of them, in 1209, that Pope Innocent III encouraged the king of Denmark to take the Cross and share in the indulgence granted to German crusaders 'to extirpate the error of paganism and spread the frontiers of the Christian faith'. This was an extraordinary statement, coming as it did from the leading apologist for crusading among the medieval popes, even though the letter did contain a reference to the persecution of Christian preachers by the heathen. It may have been a momentary aberration on Innocent's part, or on that of some clerk in his *Curia*, but it is not the only curious pronouncement he made on

10

the crusades. In 1201 he decreed that such was the need of the Holy Land that a man could take the Cross without his wife's assent. This ran counter to the traditional principle of canon law on the binding and enduring consequences of the marriage contract: no one could unilaterally refuse his partner marital rights without that partner's permission. Even Urban II had been careful to state that no young married man was to join the First Crusade without his wife's consent. Innocent had made an elementary mistake and later canon lawyers were careful to limit the exception to the sole case of the interests of the Holy Land. Innocent's statements to the king of Denmark and on a crusader's wife can perhaps only be understood in terms of his obsession with crusading, unparalleled in any pope save Gregory X and perhaps Innocent XI, which led him to preach or authorize no fewer than six crusades. It is not surprising that he overstepped the mark at times.

The opinions that vengeance for such injuries as the mere denial of the Christian faith or the refusal to accept Christian government, and the opportunity for conversion by force constituted just causes, were those of minorities and were never held by most reputable Christian thinkers, among whom it was generally agreed that non-Christians could not be made to accept baptism nor could they be physically attacked simply because they were of a different faith. And although there remained an undercurrent of belief in the missionary crusade, Pope Innocent IV authoritatively restated the conventional views in the middle of the thirteenth century. He asserted that infidels had rights in natural law and that a war of conversion was illegitimate; but he also argued that the Holy Land was rightfully Christian property, for it had been consecrated by the presence of Christ and conquered by the Roman, later to be the Christian, Empire in a just war. As representative of Christ and heir of the emperors, the pope could reassert Christian jurisdiction in Palestine and the crusades to the East were merely recovering territory that rightfully belonged to Christians. A just war, moreover, could be launched to repel unjust damage and as a punishment for sins; so the pope could proclaim a crusade against a pagan ruler, not because he was pagan but because he posed a threat to Christians or had sinned by, for example, refusing to allow Christian missionaries to operate in his territories.

Innocent's influence can be seen working particularly clearly in a treatise written by the senior Dominican Humbert of Romans for Pope Gregory X in the early 1270s. Humbert set out to answer those who said that Christians should never take the initiative but were justified only in defending themselves when the Muslims launched an attack upon them. He replied that the Muslims were dangerous and sought whenever they could to harm Christianity; they had seized lands once in the possession of Christians and they so openly consented to iniquity that no Christian could ever be at peace with them without incurring blame. The invasion of their lands was therefore justified and he argued for pre-emptive attacks upon them to weaken their power, to reintroduce the Christian faith in those lands from which it had been driven out and to express intolerance of sin. But he stressed that the crusade was not a war of aggression because its aim was the recovery of what had been Christian territory.

It has been suggested that it was only with Pope Innocent IV that the crusades were truly made subject to the Christian laws governing the use of force. But in fact the traditional criteria, even if under discussion, had weighed heavily with apologists from the start. It is striking how consistently propaganda on behalf of the crusades – whether to the East or in Spain, along the shores of the Baltic, against heretics or Christian secular powers – justified them in terms of the recovery of property or of defence against aggression.

Crusades to the Near East

A just cause was in the mind of Pope Urban II when he preached the First Crusade, a move he may have been considering for some years. In the first week of March 1095 a council of bishops from France, Italy and Germany was in session at Piacenza. To it came an embassy from the Byzantine emperor Alexius I Comnenus, appealing to the pope to encourage Westerners to help defend the Eastern church against the Turks, who had swept through Asia Minor and had almost reached Constantinople. Urban replied with a sermon in which he urged men to assist the emperor. His itinerary after Piacenza demonstrates that he set out, as he put it, to 'stimulate the minds' of the nobles and knights in his homeland, France. His year-long journey, processing crowned through country towns, which had never, or had hardly ever, seen a king in living memory, accompanied by an impressive entourage, including cardinals and senior officials of the Roman Church and a flock of French archbishops and bishops, was deliberately theatrical. Everywhere he went he dedicated cathedrals, churches and altars. He presided over councils at Clermont (November 1095), Marmoutier near Tours (March 1096) and Nîmes (July 1096), at which his already impressive entourage was greatly augmented. He first preached the crusade on 27 November in the open air, in a field outside the town of Clermont. It fell a little flat because the number of important laymen in his audience was relatively small, but that had not been his intention, for it seems that he had instructed bishops to bring with them to the council the leading nobles in their dioceses. He also preached the Cross at Limoges, Angers, Le Mans, Tours and Nîmes, and probably elsewhere besides, and he presided over Cross-taking ceremonies at Tours and possibly Le Mans. He made a detour to celebrate the feast of the Assumption at the great Marian shrine of Le Puy, the bishop of which, Adhémar of Monteil, was to be his representative on the crusade, and he celebrated the feasts of St Giles and St Hilary at St Gilles and Poitiers respectively.

It soon became clear that the response to his call was very great, greater perhaps than he had anticipated. There are many descriptions of the message he was trying to get across and although most cannot be trusted, being written in the afterglow of the capture of Jerusalem, there also survive five of his letters referring to the crusade, the text of one of the crusade decrees of the council of Clermont, together with descriptions of others, and many charters written on behalf of recruits. He called for a war of 'liberation', a word that had a particular resonance for the Church reformers who had been active for the previous half-century. He proposed two liberating goals: the liberation of people, the baptized members of the Eastern churches, and especially the Church of Jerusalem, from Muslim domination and tyranny; and the liberation of a place, the Holy Sepulchre, Christ's tomb which had reverberated with the energy released at the moment of Resurrection, within the city of Jerusalem, itself consecrated by Christ's blood and the focus of God's interventions in this world. It used to be thought that although he put forward Jerusalem as a goal to link the crusade with pilgrimages and to appeal to his listeners, his real purpose was the more limited one of fraternally complying with the request of the Byzantine emperor for aid, in the hope of bringing the Latin and Greek Churches closer together, and that it was his audience who took up the idea of the road to Jerusalem, originally a secondary, devotional aim, and fixed on it so that even before the crusade departed, the city had become the primary objective. But it is clear from the evidence of chronicles and charters connected with his preaching tour that, although aid to the Eastern Christians and the union of the Churches were also aims, Jerusalem was uppermost in his mind from the start: its name was far too potent to be used lightly by a reformer and Cluniac monk like Urban. And we now know that for some years beforehand Emperor Alexius had been writing to Western nobles, enticing them with the prospect of the liberation of Jerusalem. The justification for the crusade, therefore, was the reconquest of Christian territory, and especially Christ's own patrimony, which had been usurped by the Muslims, and the pope's appeal was presented in such a way that it conformed to the criterion of a just cause.

The crusaders broke into the Levant at a time when, coincidentally and probably unknown to them, all the dominant personalities in Baghdad and Cairo, the two nearest centres of Islamic authority, had perished, leading to the fragmentation of the empire of the Seljuk sultans who reigned in the name of the caliph in Baghdad. The crusaders were, therefore, charging through a gate which was already off its hinges, although they and their contemporaries in the West were convinced that their seizure of Jerusalem was a miraculous example of divine intervention and proof that the crusade really was what God had wanted. At any rate, with this triumph the justification for crusades to Palestine changed. The land consecrated by the presence of Christ was now in Christian hands and must be defended. Pope Eugenius III stressed this in 1145, in words which were echoed in later papal letters.

By the grace of God and the zeal of your fathers, who strove to defend them over the years and to spread Christianity among the peoples in the region, these places have been held by Christians until now and other cities have courageously been taken from the infidel . . . It will be seen as a great token of nobility and uprightness if those things which the efforts of your fathers acquired are vigorously defended by you, the sons. But if, God forbid, it comes to pass differently, then the bravery of the fathers will be shown to have diminished in the sons.

The city of Jerusalem was lost to Saladin in 1187 and was to be held by the Christians again only from 1229 to 1244. Of course its recapture came to be called for, although the burden of propaganda naturally rested on the need to defend what was left of the European settlement in the Holy Land. Even the conquest of Egypt, attempted in 1218 and 1249 and proposed at other times, was seen as contributing to the well-being of Latin Palestine. One account made King John of Jerusalem in 1218 advise the invasion of Egypt to a council of war of the Fifth Crusade:

for if we could take one of these cities [of Alexandria and Damietta] it is my opinion that by the use of it we could recover all of this [Holy] Land if we wanted to surrender it in exchange.

Since Egypt had been part of the Christian Roman Empire its occupation could also be justified as the recovery of a once Christian land.

With the loss of what remained of Christian Palestine in 1291 the recovery of the Holy Land remained a refrain until the growing threat to the Balkans from the Ottoman Turks in the later fourteenth century led the justification of crusading to change to the need to defend the European homelands themselves.

Crusades in Spain

For a long time there had been wars against the Moors in Spain and Pope Urban II tried to dissuade Spaniards from joining the First Crusade, establishing an analogy between the reconquests of the peninsula and Palestine. In 1100 and 1101 his successor Paschal II also forbade Spaniards to go to the Holy Land and granted a remission of sins to those who stayed behind to fight: he did not want military success against the Moors jeopardized by the desertion of warriors. Although it is probable that before the 1120s few Spaniards themselves equated the Reconquest with crusading, from 1098 onwards the remission of sins given to them was often equated with that granted to crusaders to Jerusalem, and in 1123 the bishops at the First Lateran Council found it possible to refer to those who took the Cross either for Jerusalem or for Spain, as though both vows were of the same kind. By the time of the Second Crusade a contemporary could write of the Spanish army as being part of one great host fighting on several fronts of Christendom.

Spain had once been Christian land, but great tracts of it were subject to Muslims, who threatened the faithful in the north. The Spanish crusades, like those to the East, were portrayed as being defensive, although it was occasionally maintained that the Reconquest would be the key to the unlocking of a route to Jerusalem by way of North Africa. In 1125, for example, the archbishop of Compostela argued that

Just as the knights of Christ ... opened the way to Jerusalem ... so we should become knights of Christ and, after defeating his wicked enemies the Muslims, open the way to the Lord's Sepulchre through Spain, which is shorter and much less laborious.

The Spanish crusades soon developed their own features. Under kings like Alfonso VIII and Ferdinand III of Castile and James I of Aragon in the thirteenth century, Alfonso XI of Castile in the fourteenth, and Ferdinand and Isabella of Spain in the fifteenth, they were also wars of national liberation under the control of the monarchs.

Crusades in North-eastern Europe

In 1147, at the time when the Second Crusade was being prepared, some German crusaders, mainly Saxons, wanted to campaign not in the Orient but against the Slavs across the river Elbe. St Bernard, who was in charge of the preaching of the Cross, agreed, perhaps because he saw in Germany similarities to Spain. He seems to have acted on his own initiative, only informing Pope Eugenius afterwards, but the pope concurred and a papal letter, *Divina dispensatione*, established the German crusade on the same lines as those in Spain and Palestine. North-eastern Europe had never been part of the Christian empire and campaigning there could not be justified as the recovery of Christian land. And it is difficult nowadays to envisage much of a threat being posed to Christendom by the backward Slav and Balt peoples; indeed, at the time relations with them were getting better. But although there was, and always had been, a missionary element in the German expeditions against their neighbours, care was also taken to justify the crusades as defensive: *dilatio* and *defensio*, expansion and defence, went hand in hand. A good example of this can be found in a letter in which Pope Innocent III authorized the Livonian Crusade in 1199. To Innocent there had been persecution of Christian converts in Livonia by their pagan neighbours. An army must therefore be raised 'in defence of the Christians in those parts' and protection was promised to all who went 'to defend the church of Livonia'.

Crusades against Schismatics and Heretics

Since very early times, the use of force against heretics had been believed to be justified, although it was considered to be a responsibility of temporal authority. Pope Gregory VII in the 1080s and the canonist Gratian in *c.*1140 laid the foundations that were to enable the church itself to authorize such violence and it was the Third Lateran Council in 1179 which first came near to proposing the launching of a crusade against heretics. The decrees of the council enjoined all the faithful for the remission of their sins to fight heresy and defend Christendom against it. It referred to such an internal action as a just labour, and stated that those taking part were to receive a remission of sins (although not automatically a plenary one) and were to be protected 'just like those who visit the Holy Sepulchre'. One result of the decree was a small expedition against the Cathars in Languedoc under the papal legate Henry of Marcy, who was later to be one of the leading preachers of the Third Crusade. A crusade can be seen functioning more certainly, with reference to schismatics, during the Fourth Crusade which, originally aimed at either Palestine or Egypt, ended by taking the Christian city of Constantinople. Already in 1203, as the expedition veered off course, there was a section of the army which was arguing for an invasion of the Byzantine Empire 'because it is not subject to the Holy See and because the emperor of Constantinople usurped the imperial throne, having deposed and even blinded his brother'. These justifications were again put forward in April 1204 when, after the emperors placed on the Byzantine throne by the Western leaders had been murdered in a *coup d'état* inside Constantinople, the army was preparing for its final assault on the city. Its clergy preached sermons justifying the attack and the burden of what they had to say was reported in almost identical passages by two eye-witnesses, Geoffrey of Villehardouin and Robert of Cléry. The clergy

> showed to the barons and the pilgrims that he who was guilty of such a murder [of the emperors] had no right to hold land and all those who had consented were abettors of the murder; and beyond all this that they had withdrawn themselves from obedience to Rome. 'For which reasons we tell you,' said the clergy, 'that this war is lawful and just and that if you have a right intention to conquer this land and bring it into obedience to Rome all those who die after confession shall enjoy the indulgence granted by the pope'.

So here was an explicit reference to the crusade conforming to the Christian criteria for war. One of the arguments, it will be noted, was that political events in Constantinople constituted a sin, an offence which the crusade could punish; in 1203 Pope Innocent had commented that such things might be so, but it was not for the crusaders to judge them nor had they assumed the Cross to vindicate this injury. The other argument was, as we would expect, that the Greeks were in schism and that this constituted active rebellion against the Church: they had 'withdrawn themselves from obedience to Rome'.

The same sort of reasoning can be found in Innocent's proclamation of the Albigensian Crusade in 1208. Already in 1204 the pope had written to King Philip II of France encouraging him to take up arms in defence of the Church against the Cathar heretics and offering the same indulgence as that granted to those who aided the Holy Land. In November 1207 he referred to the horrors of and threat from heresy, which, he averred, must be dealt with as a doctor knifes a wound, and, writing after the assassination of his legate Peter of Castelnau, on 14 January 1208, he called on Philip to take up the shield of protection of the Church. In 1215 the Fourth Lateran Council repeated that these crusaders had the right to enjoy the same indulgence as that given to defenders of the Holy Land. Similar justifications can be found on other occasions, for instance in the 1230s, when a crusade was launched in north Germany against the Stedinger peasants, who were regarded as heretics, and in the 1290s, when Pope Boniface VIII preached the Cross against his Roman rivals, the Colonnas, whom he portrayed as schismatics. Crusades against heretics and schismatics were considered to be defensive, because heresy and schism were believed to be active forces threatening the Church. To Pope Innocent III heretics were as bad as Muslims. They were a threat to Christendom, a threat, as Hostiensis put it, to Catholic unity which was in fact more dangerous than that to the Holy Land.

The redirection against enemies within Christendom of armies of penitents originally engaged to confront external threats was a novelty, particularly when men who had taken the Cross for the East found themselves being pressurized to commute their vows in favour of internal police actions. But all holy wars seem to have the tendency, whatever the religion involved, to turn inwards sooner or later and to be directed against the members of the very societies which have generated them. Peter the Venerable, the influential abbot of Cluny, was prepared to argue that violence against fellow Christians could be even more justifiable than the use of force against infidels:

> Whom is it better for you and yours to fight, the pagan who does not know God or the Christian who, confessing him in words, battles against him in deeds? Whom is it better to proceed against, the man who is ignorant and blasphemous or the man who knows the truth and is aggressive?

The belief that any chance of victory on the frontier could be vitiated by corruption or divisions at home, so that only when society was undefiled and was practising uniformly true religion could a war on its behalf be successful, was being widely expressed following the disasters which overtook the Christian settlements in Palestine in 1187. There seems to have been a correlation between failure abroad and the preaching of crusades against heresy and political opponents of the Church at home.

Crusades against Secular Powers in the West

It has often been argued, and indeed was said by some in the thirteenth century, that the least justifiable crusades were those launched against secular opponents of the papacy in Western Europe. But their roots lay back in the eleventh century, before the First Crusade, in the wars of the Investiture Controversy, a struggle between the supporters of radical church reform and its opponents, and they were justified in the traditional way; Hostiensis, indeed, was to suggest that there were no differences between the 'disobedient' and schismatics and heretics. In 1135 Pope Innocent II presided over a council at Pisa which decreed that those who fought against the pope's enemies (in this case, the South Italian Normans) 'for the liberation of the Church' should enjoy the same indulgence as that granted to the first crusaders. This development was controversial, but in 1199 another crusade was proclaimed by Innocent III against Markward of Anweiler. Markward was one of the lieutenants of Emperor Henry VI, who tried to keep control of the March of Ancona after the emperor's death and to seize the regency of the kingdom of Sicily, harassing that set up by the pope for Henry's young son Frederick II. Innocent, who was preparing the Fourth Crusade, reacted by preaching the Cross against Markward whom, he claimed, was in practice allied to the Muslims:

> We concede to all who fight the violence of Markward and his men the same remission of sins that we concede to all who go against the perfidy of the Muslims in defence of the eastern provinces, because through him aid to the Holy Land is impeded.

The pope was, in fact, proclaiming one crusade in support of another that was in preparation. The organization of the campaign against Markward was very indecisive – it has been shown that it was a measure of desperation when all else had failed – and in 1203 Markward deprived it of justification by dying, but the same train of thought can be seen in 1215 in the

Ad Liberandam constitution of the Fourth Lateran Council, according to which those who broke the peace in Europe during the crusade, holding

> ecclesiastical censure in little esteem, can fear, not without reason, lest by the authority of the Church secular power be brought in against them, as those disturbing the business of the Crucified One.

And it was probably in evidence in the authorizations of crusades in 1216–17 and 1265 against rebellious English nobles.

The next move was made by Pope Gregory IX – not in 1228–30 when his campaign against Emperor Frederick II was certainly not a crusade and should be compared more with the steps taken to defend the papacy in the eleventh century – but in 1240. War had broken out again and Frederick was now threatening the city of Rome itself. Gregory publicly exhibited the holiest relics, the heads of SS Peter and Paul, distributed crosses and called on the Roman populace to defend the liberty of the Church. His legate in Milan was permitted to preach the Cross in order to raise an army in Lombardy and crusade preaching was also authorized in Germany. A letter sent to Hungary in February 1241 listed the benefits to be granted to those taking the Cross, including the same indulgence as that given to crusaders to the Holy Land and permission to commute vows originally made for defence of Palestine to the campaign against Frederick. The defensive nature of the war was emphasized: Gregory pointed out that Christianity was 'in such peril' that military action had become necessary and he referred to the 'vows of the crusaders in defence of the Church against Frederick'. Justification in terms of defence, indeed, characterized all the appeals for the crusades against secular powers in the West. For example, a new crusade against Frederick in 1246 was proclaimed for the defence of the Catholic faith and the liberty of the Church, and a crusade against King Peter of Aragon in 1284 was preached 'in defence of the Catholic faith and also the Holy Land'.

A Cause for a Crusade

A crusade, whenever and against whomsoever it was aimed, was described as being essentially defensive and in conformity with the principle of the just cause. Of course, it has never been beyond the wit of man plausibly to excuse his actions, presenting them in the best possible light by calling attention to a threat that does not really exist, but it is undeniable that the just cause had important effects on the movement. A pope might proclaim a crusade, but success depended, as many popes found to their cost, not only on the summons but also on the response of the faithful to it. By no means all who took the Cross were altruistic, but the doubts of ordinary people worried apologists and theoreticians like Hostiensis and in an idealistic age there could be no lasting appeal that did not have a clear justification. The requirement of a just cause, therefore, was bound to be a limiting factor, for a crusade had to be presented as a reaction to past or present injury. The initiative had to lie with the enemy and a crusade was often a ponderously slow response to what the other side had done.

As far as the cause for them was concerned, crusades did more than conform to the traditional Christian criterion for the employment of force, because they had a special feature. The recovery of property or defence was related not to a particular country or empire but to Christendom at large, to the Church or to Christ himself. It was not the property of the Byzantine Empire or of the Kingdom of Jerusalem that was to be liberated or defended, but territory belonging by right to Christendom or to Christ. It was not Spaniards or Germans, but Christians, who were imperilled by the Moors and Slavs. The Cathars menaced not so much France, nor Frederick II the papal patrimony, as they threatened the Church. This is why the crusade leagues which became such a feature of the movement after 1332 should be treated as mutations, rather than as true crusades. In them crusading was adapted to the needs of emerging states. They never claimed to represent the whole of Christendom, but were defensive alliances between certain front-line powers, the forces of which were granted crusade privileges.

To understand the relationship between conventional crusading and Christendom at large we must take into account the political philosophy which dominated Western European thought at the time. Christendom had many meanings, but in political terms it was seen not merely as a society of Christians but as a universal state, the Christian Republic, transcendental in that it existed at the same time in heaven and on earth. Providing the political context in which men and women could fully develop their potential for loving God and their neighbours, it was the only true sovereign state. Earthly kingdoms had no real political validity, being at best temporal conveniences which could be considered to be its provinces. The Christian Republic – 'the kingdom of Christ and the Church' to the leaders of the First Crusade – had its possessions and its citizens. Any asset, such as territory once governed by Christians but now in the hands of outsiders, could be restored to its rule. Any threat to its subjects, whether from without or within, must be resisted. A crusade was its army, fighting in its defence or for the recovery of property lost by it. St Bernard could argue that the cause of King Louis VII of France, setting out for the East, was of importance not only to him 'but to the whole Church of God, because now your cause is one with that of all the world'. A century later Eudes of Châteauroux made the same point in one of his sermons:

> But someone says, 'The Muslims have not hurt me at all. Why should I take the Cross against them?' But if he thought well about it he would understand that the Muslims do great injury to every Christian.

In the late 1140s, when crusades were being fought at the same time on several fronts, they were seen as regiments in one Christian army.

> To the initiators of the expedition [wrote a German chronicler] it seemed that one part of the army should be sent to the eastern regions, another into Spain and a third against the Slavs who live next to us.

The universal Christian state was a monarchy, founded and ruled over by Christ, for whom in this world popes, bishops and kings acted as agents. Enemies of the commonwealth were the enemies of its king. Writers at the time of the First Crusade referred to the Muslims in the East as the 'enemies of God' and in one report of his sermon Urban II was made to say: 'It is not I who encourages you, it is the Lord. . . . To those present I say, to those absent I command, but Christ rules.' He probably hailed the crusaders as 'soldiers of Christ'; they wrote of themselves as 'the army of the Lord'. To Innocent III the crusade was an enterprise which was particularly Christ's own and those who aided the Muslims were acting against the 'interests of Christ himself and the Christian people'.

It was because of the special nature of its cause, and its association with a political order personally established for the good of mankind by Christ, that the crusade was not merely justifiable but was holy. The taking of the Cross was, therefore, much more than the performance of a patriotic duty. It was a religious obligation, for which the layman was particularly qualified. The great preacher James of Vitry spoke of the crusade as being incumbent on the Christian as military service was upon a vassal:

> When a lord is afflicted by the loss of his patrimony he wishes to prove his friends and find out if his vassals are faithful. Whoever holds a fief of a liege lord is worthily deprived of it if he deserts him when he is engaged in battle and loses his inheritance. You hold your body and soul and whatever you have from the Supreme Emperor and today he has had you called upon to help him in battle; and though you are not bound by feudal law, he offers you so many and such good things, the remission of all sins, whatever the penalty or guilt, and above all eternal life, that you ought at once to hurry to him.

The crusade, therefore, conformed to the principle of Christian war in that it was concerned above all with the recovery of lost lands and with defence. But its cause related to the

Church, to Christendom, seen as a political entity, and to Christ, the monarch of the universal Christian state. It is not surprising that those taking part saw themselves doing their duty by Christ as in other circumstances they might by their temporal lord or king.

3 *Legitimate Authority*

Papal Authorization

Christians are faced with the problem of reconciling the demands on the individual of love with the apparent need to resort to force in a sinful world. St Augustine's answer proved itself to be generally acceptable. In a private capacity no man ought ever to kill, even in his own defence; but he may be justified in doing so as a public duty. Warfare must be legitimized by a public authority, a ruler whose powers are normally considered to include the right to authorize it. A difference between crusades and other holy wars was that the ruler who legitimized them was not an emperor or king, but the pope, who claimed to be acting on Christ's behalf; and resulting from the papal initiative were the privileges enjoyed by crusaders, particularly the indulgence, which could be granted only by him.

Four popes laid the foundations for the way crusades were set in motion. Urban II created the precedent when he preached the First Crusade. Calixtus II may have issued the first crusade general letter; he certainly introduced formally the strategy of simultaneous crusading in two theatres of war. Eugenius III established that papal authorization was needed. Innocent III fixed the developed form of the indulgence. Whatever the contribution of Pope Gregory VII, who had died ten years before the First Crusade, to theory – and I shall touch on that question later – the initiative following the appeal of the Byzantine embassy to the council of Piacenza was Urban's own. There has been a move in recent years to credit the wandering preacher Peter the Hermit with the idea for the crusade, but that was not what most people believed at the time. The pope was, as a contemporary put it, the 'chief author of the expedition' and he regarded it as his own. 'We have constituted our most beloved son Adhémar, bishop of Le Puy, leader in our place of this pilgrimage and labour.' The acceptance of papal headship was expressed especially clearly in a letter written to Urban by the captains of the crusade in September 1098. They informed him of the death of Adhémar, 'whom you gave us as your vicar', and they went on:

> Now we ask you, our spiritual father, who started this journey and caused us all by your sermons to leave our lands ... to come to us and summon whomsoever you can to come with you ...

What could be better than that

> you who are the father and head of the Christian religion should come ... and yourself finish off the war *which is your own* ... If indeed you come to us and with us complete the journey begun through you all the world will be obedient to you.

The experiences of the crusaders on the march and their success, astonishing given the absence of overall leadership, their lack of supplies and the loss of their horses, convinced them and their contemporaries that they really had been fighting in Christ's cause and had been physically aided by the hand of God. But the situation in the settlements they established in the Levant remained precarious. A disaster for the Christians in northern Syria in 1119 led Pope Calixtus II, the brother of three earlier crusaders, to issue the first crusade general letter. This has been lost, but one of his letters relating to the Spanish theatre of war has survived and in the spring of 1123 his crusade was discussed, in terms of engagement in Spain as well as in the East, by the First Lateran Council. His crusade resulted in the capture of the Palestinian port of Tyre in 1124 and in King Alfonso I of Aragon's famous raid into southern Spain in the winter of 1125–6.

Then, on Christmas Eve 1144, the Muslims broke into the city of Edessa, the capital of the first Christian settlement established in the wake of the First Crusade. The news of the disaster, the first real setback for the Latins in the East, caused a great stir in the West, but what then happened is still rather mysterious. On 1 December 1145 Pope Eugenius III issued the letter *Quantum praedecessores*, but although this was addressed to King Louis VII and the nobles of France there is no evidence that it was published there. Meanwhile, Louis was already planning to lead a French expedition to the Holy Land. It may be that the pope issued *Quantum praedecessores* because he had heard of this, for Louis does not seem to have envisaged seeking papal authorization when he announced his idea to his Christmas court at Bourges. His proposal met with little response and his chief adviser, Suger of St Denis, was against it. Louis postponed a final decision until the following Easter and called for an opinion from St Bernard, who declared that he would not consider anything without consulting the pope. The result was that on 1 March 1146 *Quantum praedecessores* was reissued, with a slight change in the text which does not concern us here.

The story of the publication of *Quantum praedecessores* demonstrates two things. The first is that initiative did not always lie with the papacy. Louis VII was one of several leaders of major and minor expeditions (the most famous being his great-grandson Louis IX) who took the Cross without prompting from Rome. The second is that, whoever was responsible for the first move, papal authorization was considered to be essential at some stage: not only great passages but also the tiny enterprises, which were, increasingly after 1250, to depart backed by papal appeals and fortified by papal privileges, were authorized by papal letters. At first sight exceptions might be found in some canonists' treatment of the crusades against heretics and in the Teutonic Knights' crusading in the Baltic region. The canonists argued that a general authority to princes had already been given by the Fourth Lateran Council in 1215 and that therefore no special papal edict was required before the waging of war against heretics. But this, one must stress, was only because it was considered that papal authorization had already been granted. The same is true of the Teutonic Knights. In 1245 Pope Innocent IV granted plenary indulgences to all who went to fight with them in Prussia, whether this was in response to a specific appeal or not. This set up what has been called 'the perpetual crusade', in which hundreds of European nobles and knights took part in the fourteenth century, fighting winter and summer campaigns against the pagan Lithuanians in warfare which was embellished with the panoply of chivalric theatre, as we shall see. Here again legitimacy rested on an original papal authorization.

So these exceptions prove the rule. In 1145 *Quantum praedecessores* itself recounted how Urban,

> sounding forth as a heavenly trumpet, summoned sons of the Holy Roman Church from several parts of the world to free the eastern Church.

It went on:

> And so in the Lord we impress upon, ask and order all of you, and we enjoin it for the remission of sins, that those who are on God's side, and especially the more powerful and the nobles, vigorously equip themselves to proceed against the multitude of the infidels.

The letter may, of course, have been modelled on Pope Calixtus II's lost one, but it set the form in which crusades would thenceforward be proclaimed. The way the letters were written developed over the years, their style became more flowery and more dense and they are a good guide to the progress of crusade ideas, but they kept to the pattern in *Quantum praedecessores*, consisting of sections in which the circumstances that made a new crusade necessary were described, the appeal for

crusaders was made and the privileges to be granted to participants and supporters were listed. The greatest of them were
the letters of Innocent III's pontificate, *Post miserabile* (1198), *Ne
nos ejus* (1208) and *Quia major* (1213), which, together with the
great constitution *Ad Liberandam* of the Fourth Lateran Council
(1215), contain the most marvellous language and imagery.
And in practically every word papal authority is made clear:

> But to those declining to take part, if indeed there be by
> chance such men ungrateful to the Lord our God, we firmly
> state on behalf of the Apostle [St Peter] that they should
> know that they will have to reply to us on this matter in the
> presence of the Dreadful Judge on the Last Day of Severe
> Judgement.

We will see how unreal these pretensions were when it actually
came to directing the course of a crusade.

A feature of Christianity is that, although it teaches that all
man's actions are answerable to God and subject to an objective scale of values embodied in his laws, it divides governmen-
tal functions in this world into two distinct fields, the spiritual
and the temporal. This separation of functions is to be found
very early, even though there have been periods in which the
boundary between them has been indistinct or in which some
institution – Late Roman emperorship, the thirteenth-century
papacy, Anglican kingship – has claimed to transcend that
boundary. In spite of, and paradoxically also because of,
papal claims, at no period was the distinction between the
temporal and spiritual spheres of activity stressed more than
during the central Middle Ages.

If ever there was a secular activity it is war, and it is natural
that in Christian history its prosecution or the physical repres-
sion of heresy should have been regarded as the duties of
emperors and kings. How then could a churchman like the
pope authorize so secular an enterprise? We shall never understand the papal role in the crusading movement without first
grasping the paradox that the popes were at the same time
maintaining that the Church must run her own affairs freed

from the control of secular rulers and that they, as the most responsible ministers of Christ in the earthly part of the Christian Republic, had some measure of authority on his behalf in temporal matters.

These contradictory claims had been made with great force during the Investiture Controversy, which had begun as a dispute over Church order and reform but had rapidly escalated so that in 1076 and 1080 Pope Gregory VII had provisionally and then definitively deposed King Henry IV of Germany. In trying to remove a man from an indisputably secular office the pope had stepped across the frontier that divided spiritual from temporal jurisdiction. In the past, it is true, popes had claimed superiority to emperors, but the origin of the imperial office in the West lay in a coronation performed by a pope on Christmas Day 800 and the emperors had duties which could be interpreted as making them merely agents of the Church. It was another matter with western kingship, which had emerged from the fragmentation of the Roman Empire, owing little to the papacy, and had always been seen as a separate ministry for God. There were, moreover, no real precedents for papal intervention in the exercise of royal government other than the doubtful authorization by Pope Zacharias of the removal from office of King Childeric of the Franks in the middle of the eighth century. Gregory VII's deposition of Henry IV was an extreme act which might be said to have been in advance of the development of papal theory – too advanced to be properly understood or appreciated by contemporaries – and at the time it was a failure, because Gregory was driven from Rome by Henry's forces and died in exile. He was succeeded by Victor III and then in 1088 by Urban II, himself a strong Gregorian.

The conflict with the king of Germany went on and when Urban began his pontificate few German bishops recognized him and much of Germany and north and central Italy, including Rome, were controlled by Henry's anti-pope, Clement III. Urban set out to build up support for himself in the West and from Byzantium. By 1094 the German king was losing ground in Italy and in 1095, as the pope journeyed to

France after the Council of Piacenza, Henry's son Conrad, who had rebelled against his father, became his vassal at Cremona. Against this background his preaching of the First Crusade had a political significance. It was an important move in the Investiture Controversy for, when he called on the army of Christ to recover Christian land, Urban was, consciously or unconsciously, assuming for himself the imperial function of directing the defence of the Christian Republic at a time when he did not recognize Henry as emperor. Gregory VII had deposed a king; Urban II took over the prime duty of a temporal ruler. With these actions the popes began to take a special place for themselves at the summit of both jurisdictions.

Although it took some time for political thinkers and canon lawyers to catch up with the ideas expressed in the deposition of Henry IV and the preaching of the First Crusade, these foreshadowed what is known as the Papal Monarchy. By the early thirteenth century the pope claimed to be Christ's Vicar, a special representative unlike any other earthly ruler, the ordinary judge of all things with a plenitude of power, standing in an intermediate position between God and the two hierarchies of ecclesiastical and temporal ministers. But even with the full development of the theory the popes' powers were less than absolute. In the first place, the co-operative nature of the relationship between papal and temporal authority was still recognized: kings had their own share of government, holding a ministry for God in the exercise of which the pope would not normally interfere, for his court remained that of final appeal with an authority that could be invoked only in the last resort. Secondly, secular rulers could always act in ways in which popes would, perhaps could, not. The processes of papal jurisdiction, which were of course ecclesiastical, were not suited – and it was never pretended that they were – to the settlement of cases in temporal law. Thirdly, the popes really had no means of enforcing secular judgements even had they wanted to, for they had no effective means of imposing secular sentences. This can be seen clearly if one compares the reality of their government of the Church with the shadow of their government of the world. If there is one outstanding feature of the papacy in the central Middle Ages, it is the way it gained direct control of and elaborated the administrative apparatus of the Church. The period saw great development of the whole machinery of ecclesiastical government – of officials, courts and canon law – and the subordination of all, though never in practice quite as completely as a glance at structure would suggest, to Rome's will. But turning to the popes' relationship with the world, we find no such machinery. A pope like Innocent IV could solemnly depose a recalcitrant ruler like Frederick II, but he could only enforce his decision by resorting to the ecclesiastical apparatus, perhaps by threatening all Frederick's supporters with a sanction like excommunication. Or he could launch a crusade.

It is not surprising that the papacy should look for means by which the temporal world, so alien to itself, could be adapted to its own processes of government. An example of this can be seen in Innocent III's decretal *Novit*, which justified papal interference in temporal matters *ratione peccati*, by reason of the sin involved in them. It has often been pointed out that since sin is potentially present in almost every human act this more or less gave the pope a blank cheque to intervene whenever and in whatever case he liked. But far more important than that – indeed it was to lead to problems of interpretation later – were the legal consequences of the transfer of a case *ratione peccati* to papal jurisdiction. Now a moral question, it became subject to the ordinary processes of ecclesiastical law and jurisdiction: in other words, a temporal matter had become legally spiritual and had passed into a field in which the pope could properly operate. The crusade was another example of the same approach. A crusader was a soldier, but of a special kind, for he had taken a vow, *ipso facto* a spiritual matter, which resulted in him having the status of a pilgrim and consequently becoming, like a pilgrim, a temporary ecclesiastic, subject to Church courts. The crusade vow, therefore, had a significance which was certainly clear early in the twelfth century when the right of crusaders to answer cases in church courts was referred to. Of course, secular courts were reluctant to agree to a reduction in their rights of jurisdiction and it came to be accepted that crusaders should answer to them on feudal tenures, inheritance and major crimes; but the principle was accepted and the crusader, although engaged in a secular activity, was incorporated into the system in which papal power freely worked. By the introduction of the vow and the granting of pilgrim status Urban II had created the conditions in which a pope could have authority over a crusade and use with regard to it the existing machinery of church government.

There was another side to this, for everything, including subjection in this matter to the control of the ecclesiastical apparatus, depended on the Cross being taken. When a pope proclaimed a crusade, this was no more than an appeal to the faithful to make a vow which was essentially voluntary. He might threaten them with hell-fire but he could not force them to make it or punish them if they did not. Without their co-operation he could do nothing. It took, therefore, more than a pope to make a crusade. In the absence of a lay ruler's initiative, there had to be an adequate response to a papal appeal, and there were periods, particularly from 1150 to 1187, before the annihilation of the Christian army at the Battle of Hattin and the loss of the city of Jerusalem at last awoke the West, during which the popes and the Christian leaders in the East tried again and again with very little success to recruit crusaders for Palestine. In fact, the difficulties encountered by popes in getting crusades off the ground were daunting. In order to maximize the benefits of whatever response there might be, peace had to be made to prevail in Europe; agents had to be appointed to publicize the appeal and organize recruitment; and finance, increasingly important as time went on, had to be raised.

Peace in Christendom

Long tradition associated the Christian Republic with peace. To St Augustine, on whose writings the idea of the universal Christian state was rather inaccurately based, peace was a distinguishing feature of the true state, the City of God. It used to be thought that the crusade itself was seen as an instrument of peace, a means, closely associated with the movement for Truces of God, of directing the belligerence of French knights overseas. Given the violence that erupted once crusading magnates had left the districts they controlled, it now seems to be more likely that Truces of God were being revived at the time of the First Crusade to cope with a disorder which was inevitable and was foreseen. On the other hand, it was believed that peace in Europe and the unity of Christendom were essential preconditions for success and calls, often with reason, for truces and unity are to be found again and again in papal letters; persistent rivalry between the kings of France and England certainly hindered the raising of a crusade in the 1170s and 1180s. From 1187 onwards it was regularly maintained that success also depended on the reform of the Church. The appeals for this reached a climax with Pope Innocent III. To him the disunity of Christendom was a shameful scandal and after 1204 he believed that on the reform of a Church now united by the capture of Constantinople depended the reconquest of Jerusalem. Indeed, from the Fourth Lateran Council in the early thirteenth century to the Council of Trent in the middle of the sixteenth, every general council of the Church was officially summoned on the grounds that no crusade could achieve much without a reform of the Church and of Christendom. Innocent felt as deeply about political divisiveness, even, as we have seen, preaching the Cross against Markward of Anweiler for impeding a crusade and threatening others with the same fate. In the preamble to the general letter of 1198 which proclaimed the Fourth Crusade he seethed with powerful indignation, in a voice not heard since that of St Bernard:

> Now indeed...while our princes pursue one another with inexorable hatred, while each strives to vindicate his injuries, suffered at the hands of another, there is no one who is moved at the injury suffered by the Crucified One....Already our enemies insult us, saying, 'Where is your God, who cannot free himself or you from our hands?'

The calls of the popes for peace and unity were never very successful and the eventual failure of the crusades to hold the Holy Land has been attributed partly to the growing disinclination in the later thirteenth century of Western powers, deeply involved in their own rivalries, to assist it. This is an exaggeration of the true situation, but it is clear that by the 1280s the papacy was beginning to realize the futility of trying to organize a great expedition at a time when kings had other matters on their minds.

Preaching

No papal proclamation after the first was itself enough to move Europe. General letters had to be followed up by personal visits and constant publicity, a process known as the preaching of the Cross. It was obviously important that the popes should have control over this and therefore over recruitment. It might be supposed that they would have been only too happy with an enthusiastic response – or sometimes with any reaction at all – and it is true that Innocent III and his successors tried to make their preachers' tasks easier by granting indulgences even to those who merely listened to their sermons; it is a measure of the difficulties faced by the publicists that the amount of indulgence given to the audiences at crusade sermons was steadily increased as the thirteenth century wore on.

But there were occasions on which almost as bad for Rome as indifference in the West was the over-enthusiasm of men and women whom the popes wanted to remain at home. Urban II and his successors were not very successful when they tried to dissuade Spaniards from leaving the struggle on their own frontier to journey East and it proved to be impossible for structural reasons to prevent unsuitable non-combatants clogging up the armies if they insisted on taking the Cross. By virtue of his office Pope Urban could forbid priests to go without permission from their bishops, and monks and nuns under any circumstances – some did – but although he stated that he did not want old men, women without husbands or suitable companions and (unlike Innocent III) young married men without their wives' consent to take part, the only control he proposed was the injunction that parishioners should not commit themselves before they had taken advice from their priests. The fact was, as he must have known very well, that unsuitable lay people could not be prevented from joining pilgrimages, which had always been open to the elderly and the sick. Since a crusade was a pilgrimage there was no way it could be confined to young, healthy, male warriors. Non-combatants remained a problem, therefore, causing headaches for the crusade leaders who found themselves having to look after them. As late as the 1180s the writer Ralph Niger inveighed against those clerics, monks, women, paupers and old men who were joining up.

Preaching was never completely controlled by the papacy, because popular evangelizers have an important role in the history of the crusades. The most famous of them, Peter the Hermit, was active in central France and the Rhineland in 1095–6 and was followed East by an army which set out in advance of the main forces and was decimated by the Turks in western Asia Minor, although Peter himself and the remnants of his following were to play a significant part later in the crusade. Among his successors were Radulf, a Cistercian monk whose influence in the Rhineland worried St Bernard at the time of the Second Crusade; Stephen and Nicholas, the boys who were supposed to have launched the pathetic and mis-named Children's Crusade in 1212; and the Master of Hungary, the preacher of the Crusade of the Shepherds in 1251. Their sermons dwelt on those messianic, visionary themes, with an emphasis on the rewards of the poor, that character-ized the populist movement which underlay the crusades and occasionally erupted in migrations towards the Promised Land, which was believed to be a paradise only the under-privileged could gain. The popular movement peaked out of frustration in the thirteenth century, when the transportation of the armies by sea made it virtually impossible for the poor to join authorized crusades, since they could not afford to pay for the passage.

A greater part was played by the official propagandists among whom were, of course, the popes themselves. We have already seen Urban II following up his call at Clermont by touring much of France. In 1215 Innocent III opened the Fourth Lateran Council with a sermon which partly concerned the crusade and in 1216 he preached the Cross in central Italy; at Orvieto, as at Clermont 120 years before, the crowds were so great that he addressed them in the open air in spite of the heavy rain. In 1274 Gregory X referred to the crusade in at least three sermons at the Second Council of Lyons. But because of their responsibilities and commitments the popes could not engage in many personal appearances and they had to rely on others. At Clermont Urban II urged the bishops present to preach the Cross. It does not seem that many of them did so, but the success of the First Crusade led to a change of heart. Thereafter a stream of letters flowed from the papal *Curia* ordering bishops to preach the Cross themselves or help those sent by the popes to do so; and by the 1180s, at least in Britain, the prelates had with the assistance of the lesser clergy developed a fairly systematic procedure for crusade preaching. They were never very reliable, however, and the popes soon began to employ special agents. The best known of the early ones was St Bernard, who was used by Pope Eugenius III to preach the Second Crusade in France and Germany. The terms of Bernard's commission are not clear: he was certainly not a legate and so could not have been given powers to act in this matter as if he were the pope himself, although the success of his preaching, the force of his personality and influence he had with Eugenius clearly gave him great authority. The first use of legates in the preaching of the Cross appears to have been in 1173–4 and from then on they were often employed.

A new development came with Innocent III's pontificate. He combined the use of agents and provincial clergy by appointing local churchmen as his representatives. In 1198, when he proclaimed the Fourth Crusade, a legate was sent to France and well-known local churchmen like the famous preacher Fulk of Neuilly were allowed a free hand, but the pope also wanted two men in each province to be chosen from among the higher clergy to preach the Cross, together with a Templar and a Hospitaller. In 1208, when he tried, at least in France and Lombardy, unsuccessfully to promote a new crusade, he proposed to use much the same system, but in 1213 he introduced a more elaborate one. He himself kept an eye on the preaching in Italy, but for many provinces he appointed small groups of men – the numbers varied slightly – many of whom were bishops. He referred to them as executors, gave them the status of legates and laid down that they should live modestly, being accompanied by only a few servants. They were to preach, receive vows and, if given any donation for the Holy Land, store it in a religious house. They could appoint deputies in each diocese – in Liège and Cologne four of these were chosen – and the pope advised the bishop of Ratisbon to appoint deputies who could assemble the populace of two or three parishes to address them where they could not deal with them individually. The most successful of the executors was Oliver, the *scholasticus* of Cologne, whose preaching in that province, sometimes accompanied, it was said, by miracles, aroused great enthusiasm. Outside the scheme lay Hungary, where every bishop was to preach the Cross; Latin Syria and Palestine, where James of Vitry, the new bishop of Acre and the greatest preacher of the day, was to raise crusaders; Denmark and Sweden, where the legate, the archbishop of Lund, was to be assisted by the archbishop of Uppsala; and France, to which two legates were sent. This elaborate, perhaps overelaborate, structure does not seem to have been used again on the same scale, although, as in 1234, its details might be repeated in individual provinces. On other occasions prelates might again be asked to preach themselves or to choose men to do so, or groups of clergy, especially the Franciscans and Dominicans, might be directly appointed to publicize the crusades. There was, however, a tendency to give individual preachers the legation and wide powers. Examples are Conrad of Porto in Germany and Italy in the 1220s, Eudes of Châteauroux in France and Germany in the 1240s, and Ottobuono Fieschi over Norway, Flanders, Gascony, Britain and Ireland in 1265. Ottobuono had authority to appoint subordinate preachers, notaries and collectors. He preached some sermons himself, but generally delegated powers to whomsoever he thought fit, especially local friars.

We have detailed evidence for the form preaching took only from the thirteenth century, but it is clear that the pattern had already been established in the twelfth. Large-scale preaching tours, of the type initiated by Pope Urban II, were always theatrical, displaying the use of every technique that might create an ambience in which a spontaneous commitment to crusade would be harder to avoid. The day on which a sermon was to be delivered was often deliberately chosen. Pope Urban had timed his arrival in towns to coincide with great patronal feasts. In 1188, for his most important sermon in Germany, the legate Henry of Marcy chose the fourth Sunday in Lent, Laetare Sunday, the introit of the Mass of which begins, 'Rejoice Jerusalem and come together all you that love her. Rejoice with joy you who have been in sorrow'. In 1291 the archbishop of York, employing Dominicans and Franciscans from 13 communities, organized preaching rallies in 37 places in his diocese, to be held simultaneously on 14 September, the Feast of the Exaltation of the Cross. The site was often out of doors to achieve maximum effect. Like Pope Urban II 50 years before and Pope Innocent III 50 years later, St Bernard preached the Cross in the open air. He persuaded the king of France, who had taken the Cross privately, to appear on the dais at Vézelay beside him wearing his Cross and to stand there listening to his address. In 1096 the wandering preacher Peter the Hermit carried a letter he claimed had been sent him from heaven. A century and a half later the Master of Hungary carried a letter he claimed had been given him by the Blessed Virgin Mary. In the 1190s preachers stood before a huge canvas screen on which were painted Muslims on horseback desecrating the Holy Sepulchre.

Proceedings would begin with Mass being sung in the presence of as many senior churchmen from the region as could be collected together. Once it was over, the papal letter in which Christians were summoned to a particular crusade would be read in translation. These letters tended, therefore, to be drafted in highly emotional terms, as in the opening words of the proclamation of the Third Crusade, written after the news had arrived of the loss of the city of Jerusalem to Saladin:

> On hearing with what severe and terrible judgement the land of Jerusalem has been smitten by the divine hand, we and our brothers have been confounded by such great horror and affected by such great sorrow that we could not easily decide what to do or say; over this situation the psalmist laments and says: 'Oh God, the heathens are come into thy inheritance'.

The preacher would then launch into his homily. It was considered to be important to address as large a crowd as possible, but it was natural for preachers to dwell on themes and exempla which would appeal to nobles and knights, who were the recruits most needed. Preachers were advised to keep their sermons relatively short and certainly none of those which survive are particularly long. They are very scriptural, with passages of exegesis interspersed with homely anecdotes. Each ended with an *invitatio*, an appeal in which the preacher implored his listeners to take the Cross. We can get some idea of how passionate these could become from the report of a sermon preached in Basel by Abbot Martin of Pairis on 3 May 1200:

> And so, strong warriors, run to Christ's aid today, enlist in the knighthood of Christ, hasten to band yourselves together in companies sure of success. It is to you today that I commit Christ's cause, it is into your hands that I give over, so to speak, Christ himself, so that you may strive to restore him to his inheritance, from which he has been cruelly expelled.

As the *invitatio* ended a choir would strike up with a hymn or chant: in 1100 the archbishop of Milan had made use of the popular song '*Ultreia, ultreia*'. This must have been sung as men came forward to commit themselves. As each made his vow he was presented with a cloth cross, which he was supposed to have attached to his clothes at once. This aspect of the proceedings needed careful preparation, because otherwise there would have been confusion; at Vézelay in 1146 so great was the enthusiasm that the stock of made-up crosses ran out and St Bernard had to tear his habit into strips to provide additional ones. In 1463 Cardinal Bessarion issued the following instruction to preachers:

> The manner of fixing on the sign [of the Cross] shall be identical in all . . . places and shall be set in motion as rapidly as possible. When a sign has been made from red silk or cloth, they shall attach it to the breast with a pin. Those receiving it may afterwards sew it firmly in place.

Crusaders were expected to go on wearing their crosses until they came home with their vows fulfilled.

One has the impression that Cross-taking ceremonies could be highly emotional, hysterical and turbulent. Expressing themselves in terms which they hoped would strike home and seeking binding commitments, which must have often been regretted later, to a demanding, expensive and unpleasant exercise, the preachers sometimes aroused forces the Church could never have controlled:

> I address fathers and sons and brothers and nephews. If an outsider were to strike you down would you not avenge your blood-relation? How much more ought you to avenge your God, your father, your brother, whom you see reproached, banished from his estates, crucified!

It is not surprising that crusading was punctuated, particularly early on, with pogroms against Jews, ethnic cleansing and collapses in discipline.

Finance

Crusades were expensive and tended to become more so as the costs of war increased. Pope Urban II, recognizing that cash was going to be a problem, had called on the rich to help the less well-off, and great lords on the First Crusade like Duke Robert of Normandy and Count Raymond of St Gilles had subsidized knights in their contingents. It became usual for those who could afford it to pay inducements to, or a part of the expenses of, their followers. The total cost of the crusade of 1248–54 to King Louis IX of France was estimated at 1,537,570 *livres* or more than six times his annual income; and this was certainly an underestimate, as it can be shown that he spent over 1,000,000 *livres* in Palestine after his disastrous campaign in Egypt was over. But there were always knights who had to pledge or sell land to pay their way and there is evidence of their growing reluctance to meet the bills alone. Quite early on it became clear that sources of finance other than crusaders' pockets would have to be tapped.

Rulers soon came to demand subsidies from their subjects. In 1146 Louis VII imposed on France a general census to raise money for the Second Crusade; it is not clear what form this took, but it was charged on the Church as well as the laity and may have been a forced feudal levy. In 1166 a tax for the Holy Land, based on the value of movable property and income, was collected by Louis and Henry II of England. In 1185 Henry and Philip II of France levied a graduated tax on income and movables and demanded a tenth of the alms left by those who died in the ten years following 24 June 1184. They followed this in 1188 by imposing the famous Saladin Tithe for one year on the income and movables of those, clerks and laymen, who did not take the Cross. In June 1201 the papal legate Octavian persuaded John of England and Philip of France to contribute a fortieth of a year's income from their lands and to raise the same from the estates of their vassals. These occasional taxes are to be found throughout the thirteenth century. Louis IX of France, for example, pressed towns to give him money for his crusade in the 1240s and the English parliament granted the Lord Edward a twentieth of a year's income in 1270. In 1274 Pope Gregory X demanded (with what success is not known) that every temporal ruler levy from each subject one silver penny.

Alms and legacies, given from the first and particularly in the outburst of popular enthusiasm which had followed the conquest of Palestine, provided another valuable source of finance. The popes ordered chests to be placed in churches for their collection and from the middle of the twelfth century granted indulgences, though not plenary ones, to those who contributed to the movement in this way, while at the same time encouraging the faithful to make bequests to the Holy Land in their wills.

The popes themselves naturally played the most important part in the financing of crusades. They exploited the normal judicial processes of the Church – under Gregory IX and Gregory X the proceeds of fines imposed on blasphemers were sent to the Holy Land – but they also took new measures. They began to allow the redemption of crusade vows for money payments. Several trains of thought led to this development. First, the belief that all should contribute in some way was reflected in the growing practice of granting indulgences in return for donations rather than participation. Secondly, the Church was faced by large numbers who were incapable of fighting but had taken the Cross, although there was little it could do about them, as we have seen. Thirdly, churchmen and canon lawyers had to deal with those who had taken the Cross in the first flush of enthusiasm and then wanted to be dispensed from their vows. As early as the tenth century it had been considered possible to send someone in one's place on pilgrimage and in the twelfth century, while it was difficult to get relaxation from the obligations of a crusade vow, it was not impossible; indeed, it seems to have become quite common by the time of the Third Crusade.

From the pontificate of Alexander III onwards popes in decretals and canon lawyers in their commentaries began to consider dispensation, substitution (the sending of another in place of the crusader), redemption (dispensation in return for a money payment) and commutation (the performance of another penitential act in place of the one originally vowed). In the early years of his pontificate Innocent III laid down some general rules. These were exceptionally severe in that they

confirmed the Roman law concept of the hereditability of vows
– a son must perform a vow undertaken and not fulfilled by his
father – but they also stated that the pope (though only he)
could grant delay in the performance of a crusade vow or its
commutation or redemption. The amount to be paid in redemption should equal the sum that would have been spent
had the crusader actually gone with the expedition. The influence of these rulings can be seen working from 1213 onwards
in papal letters and the conciliar decree *Ad liberandam* (1215),
which referred to commutation, redemption and deferment. It
was also apparent in the actions of Robert of Courçon and
Archbishop Simon of Tyre, the legates responsible for the
preaching of the Fifth Crusade in France, who encouraged
everyone, whatever his or her health or state, to take the Cross,
in order that moneys could be raised from the subsequent
redemptions. This caused scandal, but from 1240 onwards,
in spite of papal admonitions, redemptions were being granted
almost as a matter of course to anyone who asked for them or
paid for them, although for a short period, following the loss of
Palestine in 1291, they became much harder to obtain.
Finance from them became very important as the thirteenth
century progressed, but the system was open to great abuse
and came in for much criticism – and it was only made worse
by the half-hearted attempts of some popes to reform it.

The greatest financial contribution came from the direct
taxation of the Church by the popes: a substantial part of
Louis IX's expenses were paid for by the French clergy. The
first hint of new ideas on this issue is to be found in letters
written in 1188 by Pope Clement III to the clergy of Canterbury and Genoa, encouraging them to direct some of their
wealth to the support of the crusade. Ten years later Innocent
III ordered the prelates of Christendom to send men and
money to the Fourth Crusade and he repeated this injunction
in his letter *Quia major* of 1213, but meanwhile, in December
1199, he had taken a momentous step. He had come to the
conclusion that there was nothing for it but to impose a tax
upon the whole Church, although, obviously worried about
the possible reaction from the bishops, he assured them that

this was not to become custom or law or establish a precedent, and he informed them that he himself would send a tenth of his revenues to the aid of the East. He ordered the clergy to pay a fortieth of all their revenues, after deducting anything owed in unavoidable usurious contracts; a few religious were allowed to pay a fiftieth. Provincial councils were to discuss the matter and within three months a council in each diocese was to organize collection with the aid of a Templar and a Hospitaller. With the advice of the same two brothers and local worthies each prelate was to hire soldiers and provide poor crusaders with subsidies.

The levy proved to be extremely difficult to raise. By 1201 it had been gathered neither in England nor in France and in 1208 it had not been collected even in parts of Italy. Although in 1209 Innocent III laid a tax on the churches in the domains of crusaders planning to march against the Cathars, it must have been the failure of the measure of 1199 that persuaded him not to ask for another levy in 1213. But two years later, a twentieth for three years was demanded of the Church by the Fourth Lateran Council and, although again emphasis was placed on the pope's own contribution, a general council had now confirmed his right to tax the clergy. From this time onwards income taxes were built up into a regular system, the most extensive of them, a sexennial tenth from which none was to be exempt, being promulgated in 1274 at the Second Council of Lyons. Usually apportioned at a tenth, they were demanded of the universal Church or of the clergy in a single country for periods varying from one to six years. Settlement was normally sought in two equal instalments each year, although resistance was common and the payments were nearly always in arrears. At first the proceeds were paid to local crusaders or sent directly to the Holy Land, while the popes simply received accounts, but in 1220 Pope Honorius III was already overseeing the transmission of the monies. By the middle of the thirteenth century it had become customary for the popes to grant the yield of the taxes to kings or lords who had promised to go on crusade; if the king did not then depart, the money, which had been deposited for him in monasteries, was delivered to papal merchants for sending to Rome. But such was the resistance of the temporal authorities to this practice that the popes seldom received all they should.

Enormous sums were raised from alms, bequests, redemptions and taxes and there was a need for efficient machinery for their collection. In 1188 Pope Clement III had ordered bishops to appoint clerks to collect the money and spend it on troops, but in 1198 Innocent III himself chose collectors from among the churchmen in each province; it was typical of his methods that although these were local men they were instituted directly by him. In the following year he left the organization of his new tax on the clergy to the bishops, perhaps to assuage local feelings, but the lack of co-operation soon led to officials being sent from Rome to oversee collection and Innocent returned to central control in 1213: his preachers in the provinces were also to be involved in the raising of money. Papal commissioners were put in charge of the new twentieth levied on the Church in 1215 and the whole system was carried further by Innocent's successors. In 1274 all Christendom was divided into 26 districts administered by collectors and sub-collectors. The taxes of 1199 and 1215 were assessed by the clergy themselves, but in 1228 Pope Gregory IX ordered the papal collectors to choose for this task special deputies who were to compel local churchmen under oath to value clerical incomes in a district.

Preaching and finance were two fields in which the popes could make use of the highly developed church bureaucracy and we can trace the emergence of a characteristically elaborate machinery to act on their behalf. But their problems did not end with the recruitment of crusaders and the raising of money to subsidize them. Where was a crusade to go? And how was it to be controlled on the way?

Strategy

Crusading strategy was a moral matter. Christian wars had to be fought in ways that would achieve their ends most painlessly

48

if they were to accord with the Augustinian criteria. Of course, in the conditions of the time and given the near impossibility of co-ordinating the movements of contingents from different parts of Europe, long-term planning could often present crusaders with nothing more than some general guidelines. Events in the field would always overtake plans made in the West and the final decisions had to be left to councils of war held on the spot. In 1238 the Christian leaders in Palestine suggested to Thibaut of Champagne that the fleet bringing his crusade ought to apply to Limassol in Cyprus, where it could refit and revictual. Here, a council of war would discuss whether it was best to proceed to Syria or to Egypt; Limassol, they pointed out, was equally distant from Acre, Alexandria and Damietta. Although in the 1240s King Louis IX of France had made plans to invade Egypt from the start, he did not give the final orders until his arrival in Cyprus. Some general planning, however, was made in the West. Pope Innocent III began the practice of receiving frequent reports from local Christians on political conditions in the East – he certainly took advice from them when making plans for the Fifth Crusade – and from the 1270s onwards there survive many memoranda written for the popes, most of which were composed in the early fourteenth century when the Christians had lost the Holy Land and a major effort was needed to recover it.

A revealing insight into discussions on strategy can be found in King James I of Aragon's description of a debate at the Second Council of Lyons in 1274, in which both he and Pope Gregory X took part. Present were leaders of the military orders and experienced crusaders, among whom there seems to have been general agreement that large, elaborately organized crusades were expensive, difficult to provision and support and did little long-term good; this did not prevent Gregory himself from planning a major new crusade, although he died before his preparations were complete. After 1291, crusading to the East had two goals: the recovery of Jerusalem and the defence of the remaining Latin settlements in Greece and the Greek islands, especially against the piratical activities of the Turks. Inevitably, the second of these (which had more practical significance) took over from the first and in 1332 there came into being the first 'crusade league', a naval alliance of independent powers, designed to confront the Turkish pirate emirates. Henceforward, crusading was to be as much a naval as a military affair and, as the threat from the Ottoman Turks grew and crusading became more a matter of defending Europe itself, naval leagues were to play an important part in the defence of Christendom.

Control

The crusades were papal instruments, the most spectacular expressions of the Papal Monarchy, the armies of the Christian Republic marching in response to calls from the men who on earth represented its monarch. We have seen that popes faced great difficulties in promoting and financing them, but once an army had been collected together, the logistic problems solved and a goal set, the troops had to be controlled at a distance and this was the most difficult task of all. From the start the popes were represented on crusades by legates. A legate would be appointed to supervise the whole army, but there could also be subordinate legates chosen to oversee national or regional contingents, though their relationship with their superiors was not always easy: on the Second Crusade, Arnulf of Lisieux and Godfrey of Langres, each assisted by a man from his diocese, were papal representatives with the Anglo-Norman and French crusaders, but did not get on well with Theodwin and Guy, who had responsibilities for the whole expedition. Legates were always churchmen and herein lay an insuperable problem. The popes and their representatives were priests and as such were forbidden by canon law to take up arms and fight. The military direction of crusades should not, therefore, be entrusted to them. This was expressed particularly clearly in c.1150 by St Bernard, who wrote to Pope Eugenius III after being approached to lead a new crusade. How could he command military forces? It was now time, he wrote, to draw the two swords, spiritual and temporal, at the pope's disposal. Both St Peter's swords had to be drawn, one by his hand, but the other at his command, for it seemed that Peter himself was not personally to wield the temporal weapon, as he had been ordered by Christ on the eve of the crucifixion to put up his sword into its scabbard.

One legate whose powers have been studied closely is Adhémar of Le Puy, appointed 'leader' of the First Crusade. The general conclusion seems to be that to Pope Urban Adhémar's leadership was to be understood not as military captaincy but in the context of spiritual duties, expressed through advice, arbitration and exhortation. The limitations on Adhémar's powers of command are paralleled over and over again in the history of the crusades. The Fourth Lateran Council decreed that priests in the Christian army

> should diligently devote themselves to prayers and exhortations, teaching the crusaders both by word and example, so that they may always have before their eyes Divine Fear and Love and do not say or do anything that offends the Divine Majesty.

Pope Innocent III wrote with regard to another legate: 'As Joshua fights he ascends with Aaron the Mount of Contemplation and prays.' Of course, there were exceptions, like Pelagius of Albano in the thirteenth century and Peter Thomas and Gil Albornoz in the fourteenth, men whose strength of personality and energy led to them assuming military command. In general, however, crusading practice followed canon law, which made the pope and his legate dependent on the goodwill and competence of the secular leaders, who alone would exercise military command. Over the most potent expression of his temporal claims a pope had very little control once an army was on the move, and he could only watch helplessly if it was carried off course.

This point is illustrated by the events which led to the assault by the Fourth Crusade upon the Byzantine Empire. There has been much debate on this diversion and all sorts of theories have been put forward to explain it. The least acceptable was that which made Innocent III a party to a plot in the West to divert the crusade to Constantinople, for it credited him with far more power than he actually possessed. One must not confuse what he did after the expedition was over with his attitude before and during it. There is no doubt that a very short time after the capture of Constantinople he was engaged in an all-out effort to subordinate the Greek Church to Rome. In his demands for conformity he was doing something new – such a rigorous attitude towards the Eastern Churches had not hitherto been found in the Latin settlements in the East – but his acceptance and exploitation of a novel situation should not be taken as evidence that from the start he was involved in plans to conquer Greece. We have seen that he was obsessed by the crusades and by the need to help the Holy Land. In the years 1202 to 1204 he was also comparatively young and inexperienced. Faced by ruthless politicians, who actually prevented his legate Peter Capuano from joining the crusade at Venice, and by a leviathan that went lumbering away out of control, his compliance and long silences, which have aroused suspicion, can surely best be interpreted as hesitation, an inability to decide how to put his precious instrument back on its right path.

We have seen that the authority which legitimized this form of holy war was the papacy; that the crusaders' vows enabled a temporal activity to be brought under some ecclesiastical authority; that the popes could act with effect in the proclamation, preaching and financing of a crusade; but that their control over recruitment was limited and that once the army was on the march their powers were more theoretical than real. No spiritual leader, however exalted, could really manage so secular an affair as war.

4 *Who Were the Crusaders?*

The Vow

There could be no crusade without crusaders and what made a man or woman a crusader was the making of a vow, which was introduced by Pope Urban II. At Clermont, the pope asked his audience to make promises and told those who answered his call to sew crosses on their clothes as a sign of their commitment. The vow was a new element in the Christian Holy War, although it was the product of a train of thought already in Urban's mind before November 1095. At Piacenza in the previous March he had replied to the appeal from the Greeks by urging men to take an oath to help God and the Byzantine emperor against the Muslims. Christian vows had had a long history and for a long time had been viewed as creating legally binding obligations, but over the next century and a half they were to be treated exhaustively by canon lawyers. They came to be defined as deliberate commitments made to God to do or not to do certain acts. They could be simple, made with no formalities and therefore not enforceable as far as the Church was concerned, or solemn, publicly taken, expressed in the present tense and legally binding. They could be general, obligatory on all Christians, or special, resulting in individual, voluntary acts; necessary, in that they were needed for salvation, or voluntary, undertaken out of personal devotion; pure, being absolute commitments, or conditional. A man would go through several stages – termed *deliberatio*, *propositum* and *votum*

– before he was definitely committed, but once he had made a *votum* this, if unfulfilled, was binding on his heirs, although in certain circumstances he could be dispensed from it or could commute it.

The definition just given was the product of a long period of development, but it is a useful starting-point from which to describe the vow to crusade. This was usually solemn, always special and voluntary and often conditional. It resulted in a temporary commitment which, in relation to the twelfth-century expeditions to the East, may have been to visit the Holy Sepulchre in Jerusalem, with the qualification that the pilgrimage must be made in the ranks of an organized armed expedition authorized by the pope. Surviving evidence for the Albigensian Crusade suggests that in that case the vow was made to war against the heretics and enemies of the faith in Languedoc.

By the later twelfth century vows of crusaders and pilgrims were believed to be closely related. From the first the obligation of crusaders had been to make what was regarded as a pilgrimage; some of their privileges had previously been enjoyed by pilgrims and they were usually invested with the scrip and staff of pilgrims as well as with the Cross that marked their special promise. It is doubtful, however, whether many pilgrims to Jerusalem before the First Crusade had made vows. They had been, broadly speaking, of three types. The first were those performing penances imposed on them by their confessors. By the thirteenth century this category had been defined and further subdivided into three, depending on the nature of the sin and the status of the confessor. No vow was needed to perform an enjoined penance. The second, often hard to distinguish from the first because there was a penitential element in their journeys as well, were those engaged in what was called a *peregrinatio religiosa*, an act of devotion undertaken voluntarily and perhaps vowed, but not enjoined by a confessor. The third were those who were going to Jerusalem to live there until they died; the special position of the city in the geography of providence meant that it was a place in which devout Christians wanted to be buried. In introducing the vow for all, together with the concept of penitential war to which I will turn in a moment, Urban was, in effect, creating a new type of pilgrimage, like the *peregrinatio religiosa* in that it was volunteered out of devotion, but also like the penitential one in that its performance constituted a formal penance and was set by him in the context of the confessional. In some ways, however, the old pattern survived. There were always to be crusaders who had been enjoined to take the Cross by their confessors and who were, therefore, more like the first kind of eleventh-century pilgrim, and by 1200 a distinction was being made between a crusade enjoined by a confessor and one volunteered out of devotion, although the vow had become a prerequisite for all.

Penitents

The defining, and most radical, feature of a crusade was that it was penitential. Merit had been attached to war for several centuries and it was not hard for Urban to declare that fighting in a just cause as a soldier of Christ was a positive act of virtue, an expression of love both of God, for whom one fought, and of one's neighbours in the Eastern Churches, whom one was striving to liberate. He stressed – references appear in all the reports of his sermons – the difference between the old unregenerate knight, who quarrelled with his neighbours, and the new knight, who fought for such a worthy cause:

> Now become soldiers of Christ you who a little while ago were robbers. Now legally fight against barbarians, you who once fought against brothers and blood-relations...Those who were the enemies of the Lord, now these will be his friends.

The impact of the comparison between the old and new knight on audiences is borne out by the way it was repeated by preachers for a century. St Bernard, in particular, concentrated on it. To him the old knight committed homicide,

55

whether he lived or died, prevailed or was conquered; the new knight killed not man, but evil:

> For how long will your men continue to shed Christian blood; for how long will they continue to fight amongst themselves? You attack one another, you slay one another and by one another you are slain. What is this savage craving of yours? Put a stop to it now, for it is not fighting but foolery. So to risk both soul and body is not brave but shocking, is not strength but folly. But now O mighty soldiers, O men of war, you have a cause for which you can fight without danger to your souls; a cause in which to conquer is glorious and for which to die is gain.

But Urban had gone further. He had proposed that a crusader would be engaged in this war as a means of grace for the remission of all his sins; and the phrase *remissio peccatorum*, echoing the Nicene Creed's definition of baptism, could hardly have had a more potent sound to it. Although the first grant of a remission of sins to fighters has been attributed to Pope Alexander II and has been associated with knights going to besiege Barbastro in Spain in 1063–4, grave doubts have been expressed whether Alexander's words should be interpreted in this way. The first certain expression of the idea of penitential war emerged nearly 20 years later out of a dialogue between Pope Gregory VII and a group of scholars in the entourage of Countess Mathilda of Tuscany, one of the most zealous and belligerent of his supporters. It was unprecedented in Christian history and it was revolutionary, in that it put the act of fighting on the same meritorious plane as prayer, works of mercy and fasting. Gregory's reasoning seems to have been that the act of fighting in a just cause was penitential because it was arduous and exposed the individual concerned to danger.

This created a new category of warfare. For a time crusading was to be one of several manifestations of it – although the most important – but like so much of the radical thought bubbling to the surface during the Investiture Controversy, the notion of going to war as a penance would have been hard to defend on theological grounds. It would never have been easy to justify the inflicting of pain and loss of life (with the consequential distortion of the perpetrator's internal dispositions), as penitential simply because the penitent was exposing himself to danger, however unpleasant the experience might have been for him. It was to be Urban's achievement to give the idea a context in which it could be presented more convincingly, because he associated it with the most charismatic of all traditional penances, the pilgrimage to Jerusalem.

The idea caught the imagination of contemporaries, although it must have worried senior churchmen like Anselm of Canterbury and Ivo of Chartres. Crusaders believed that they were embarking on a campaign in which their obligations, at any rate if completed, would constitute for each of them that act of self-punishment which a penance was regarded as being. A penitential ambience pervaded their campaigning, giving it an entirely different colouring from other expressions of Holy War. Whereas in them the soldier's service involved passive obedience to God's command, in crusading he was invited to co-operate actively, because everything depended on his decision to undertake the penance of fighting. This is why St Bernard and other preachers dwelt on the opportunities the crusade provided for the sinner:

> [God] puts himself into a position of necessity, or pretends to be in one, while all the time he wants to help you in your need. He wants to be thought of as the debtor, so that he can award to those fighting for him wages: the remission of their sins and everlasting glory. It is because of this that I have called you a blessed generation, you who have been caught up in a time so rich in remission and are found living in this year so pleasing to the Lord, truly a year of jubilee.

It is no exaggeration to say that a crusade was for the early crusader as an individual only secondarily about service in arms to God or the benefiting of the Church or Christianity; it was primarily about benefiting himself, since he was engaged in an act of self-sanctification.

So the knights of Christ fought in expiation of their sins and as a means to their salvation. They were, in the Old Testament imagery constantly used of them, the elect, the Israelites crossing the Red Sea. They were expected to conform to such standards of behaviour and dress as were suitable for members of the Lord's host, and papal and secular decrees contained what are known as sumptuary clauses demanding simplicity of dress and temperance in daily life:

> And if at any time the crusaders should lapse into sin, may they soon rise again through true penitence, having humility in heart and body, following moderation both in clothing and in food, shunning altogether quarrels and envy, banishing inward rancour and anger, so that, fortified with spiritual and material weapons, they may do battle with the enemy, more secure in faith, not presuming on their own power but trusting in divine strength.

A mid-twelfth-century sculpture of a man and his wife, which once stood in the cloister of the priory of Belval in Lorraine, portrays the man wearing simple travelling garments, although his staff and purse – the symbols of pilgrimage – and the Cross sewn on the front of his cloak show him to have been a crusader.

The penitential nature of crusading explains why, after the often revolting violence, the most characteristic feature of any expedition was how liturgical it was. The first crusaders began each new stage of the march barefooted and fasted before every major engagement. In June 1099 they processed solemnly around the city of Jerusalem, which was still in Muslim hands:

> The bishops and priests, barefoot and dressed in sacred vestments with crosses in their hands, went from the Church of St Mary on Mt Sion to the Church of the protomartyr St Stephen, singing and praying that the Lord Jesus Christ deliver his holy city and Holy Sepulchre...The clergy, dressed in this way, and the armed knights and their followers processed side by side.

Fasts and processions featured in all crusades, but penitential liturgy was not confined to the expeditions. Crusaders knew that while they were on campaign a column of prayer would be rising up to heaven from Western Europe, both intercessory, on their behalf, and penitential, because failure in God's war would result as much from the faults of men and women on the home front as from those of the fighters.

> It is incumbent upon all of us [wrote Pope Gregory VIII in 1187] to consider and to choose to amend our sins by voluntary chastizement and to turn to the Lord our God with penance and works of piety; and we should first amend in ourselves what we have done wrong and then turn our attention to the treachery and malice of the enemy.

As early as 1100 the archbishop of Rheims wrote to one of his suffragans, announcing the fall of Jerusalem to the crusaders and ordering that in all parishes there should be prayers for victory, fasting and the collection of alms. In 1213 a new element was introduced into the rite of the Mass by Pope Innocent III. Before the *Pax* all men and women were to prostrate themselves on the ground while Psalm 79 (78) – 'Oh God, the heathen are come into thy inheritance' – was to be sung or said, followed by a prayer for the liberation of the Holy Land. These liturgical intercessions became widespread and very common.

The Indulgence

Catholics believe that after confession, absolution and the performance of the works that earn it, a sinner is granted by the Church on God's behalf remission of all or part of the penalties that are the inevitable consequence of sin. When all penalties are remitted the indulgence is called 'plenary'. The remission applies not only to the punishment imposed by the Church itself, usually by a priest in the confessional, but also to the temporal punishment imposed by God either in this world or the next. A question that concerned the crusaders from the first, and also canon lawyers, who were trying to assuage their worries in the thirteenth century, was whether the indulgence was effective from the moment the Cross was taken or only once the crusade had been accomplished; in other words, was it consequent upon the making of the vow or on the performance of the act for which the vow was made? This was important since upon a ruling hung the hopes of heavenly reward for crusaders who died before completely fulfilling their vows or even before they had begun to carry them out. St Thomas Aquinas was of the opinion that the wording of the papal grants of indulgence was vital here: if an indulgence had been conceded to those who took the Cross 'for the aid of the Holy Land', the condition of the indulgence was merely the making of the vow and not the journey; if, on the other hand, an indulgence had been given specifically to those who were going overseas, then the condition, the crusade itself, must be fulfilled before it could be effective. But there was no general agreement on the matter.

The indulgence, as we know it, was not fully developed until the thirteenth century. The First Crusade was preached at a time when the Church's penitential teaching was altering. In the late tenth century the Carolingian penitential pattern – confession, satisfaction for sin through penance and only then reconciliation through absolution – had begun to change, a process that was assisted by the introduction of the practice of reconciling the sinner after confession but before he had made satisfaction by undergoing his penance. This led to the distinction, made by Hugh of St Victor and Gratian in the twelfth century, between the guilt of sin, ended through reconciliation, and the punishment due for it. But it also made men and women anxious about satisfaction, because after absolution in the confessional they were still conscious of a burden of punishment remaining. This would, of course, be expiated in the performance of penance, but that penance would no longer be formally confirmed by a priest as having been satisfactory. More fundamentally, developments in contemporary theology were leading them to doubt whether any penances done by them as human beings could ever make full satisfaction to God and so divine punishment in this world or the next weighed even more heavily on their minds. They sought God's mercy and they looked to works other than their own which might contribute to their salvation. One consequence was the doctrine of the Treasury of the Church, according to which an inexhaustible credit-balance of merit had been stored up by Christ and the saints on which the Church could draw on behalf of a repentant sinner. This doctrine came to be fully formulated in the thirteenth century, but was present in an embryonic form much earlier.

So, by the late eleventh century, two attitudes to penance co-existed. The first, the old view, was that a penance, if it was severe enough – a six-month fast on bread and water, for example, or a pilgrimage on foot to Rome – could make satisfaction to God for sin. The second was that it was doubtful whether any penance could ever be satisfactory and that the sinner had to rely on God's mercy to make good any deficiency by rewarding the devout performance of a meritorious work with a release from punishment. It was the old view that was expressed in the earliest 'indulgences', among them Pope Urban II's grant of full remission of sins to the first crusaders in 1095. It has been suggested, on the basis of what seem to be contradictory phrases in Urban's letters, describing on the one hand a relaxation of penance imposed in the confessional and on the other a remission of sins, that the preachers of the Cross went further than Urban had intended or even that the pope himself was confused. But there is no hint in the sources that contemporaries saw any contradictions. The decree of the Council of Clermont, in which 'Whoever for devotion alone, not to gain honour or money, goes to Jerusalem to liberate the Church of God can substitute this journey for all penance', and Urban's apparently indiscriminate references to the 'remission of all penances' and the 'remission of all sins', were in fact expressions of the same idea, that the crusade as an armed pilgrimage to Jerusalem was so rigorous, painful and dangerous an exercise that it would purge the participants of their past crimes. Accounts of the crusade contained references to the crusaders being 'cleansed of their sins', 'purged and reconciled to God' and 'reborn through confession and the penance which you undergo daily in hard labour'. It is clear from an explanation of Urban's motives, given four decades later by the historian Orderic Vitalis, that whether granting release from *all* penances – presumably those not completely fulfilled in the past as well as those that might have been imposed in confessionals on the eve of the expedition – or remitting *all* sins, the pope was declaring authoritatively that a crusader would make adequate satisfaction to God by taking part in such a severely penitential act.

The papacy has generally been conservative in its theology and the increasingly old-fashioned idea that a crusade was in its very severity an adequately satisfactory penance, and that the pope was making an authoritative pronouncement to that effect, prevailed in papal thinking almost to the end of the twelfth century. As late as 1187, in the letter *Audita tremendi* which launched the Third Crusade, Pope Gregory VIII wrote that

> to those who with contrite hearts and humbled spirits undertake the labour of this journey and die in penitence for their sins and with right faith we promise full indulgence of their faults and eternal life; whether surviving or dying they shall know that through the mercy of God and the authority of the apostles Peter and Paul and our authority they will have relaxation of the satisfaction imposed for all their sins, of which they have made proper confession.

That this was an old-fashioned assurance that the penitential nature of the exercise would be satisfactory was made clear by the contemporary apologist Peter of Blois when he wrote that

> by the privilege of the apostle Peter and the general authority of the Church the Lord had intended in this sign [of the Cross] a means of reconciliation; so that the assumption of the commitment to journey to Jerusalem should be the highest form of penance and sufficient satisfaction for sins committed.

The second, and increasingly popular, view that satisfaction could never be adequate but that God could mercifully treat inadequate penances as though they were satisfactory, and that a free and generous remission of all punishment – detached, in a sense, from the nature of the penance performed – could be granted by the pope on God's behalf, was already implicit in the writings of St Bernard at the time of the Second Crusade:

> Take the sign of the Cross and the supreme pontiff, the vicar of him to whom it was said, 'Whatever you loose on earth will be loosed in heaven', offers you this full indulgence of all the sins you confess with contrite hearts.

The emphasis on God's mercy and on rewards rather than on satisfaction for sin is also to be found in Pope Eugenius III's *Quantum praedecessores*, perhaps written under Bernard's influence:

> By the authority of omnipotent God and that of Blessed Peter the prince of the apostles, conceded to us by God, we grant remission of and absolution from sins, as instituted by our aforesaid predecessor [Urban II], in such a way that whosoever devoutly begins and completes so holy a journey or dies on it will obtain absolution from all his sins of which he has made confession with a contrite and humble heart; and he will receive the fruit of everlasting recompense from the rewarder of all.

But the approach of Bernard and Eugenius was exceptional before the pontificate of Innocent III. It was in Innocent's *Post miserabile*, proclaiming the Fourth Crusade in 1198, that there appeared for the first time the fully developed indulgence, which was now definitively adopted by the papacy.

> We, trusting in the mercy of God and the authority of the blessed apostles Peter and Paul, by that power of binding and loosing that God has conferred on us, although unworthy,

63

grant to all those submitting to this labour personally and at their expense full forgiveness of their sins, of which they have been moved to penitence in voice and heart, and as the reward of the just we promise them a greater share of eternal salvation.

As an unequivocal assurance of divine recompense it made a great impression. The crusader Geoffrey of Villehardouin wrote that

> because the indulgence was so great the hearts of men were much moved; and many took the Cross because the indulgence was so great.

And James of Vitry's treatment of the indulgence in one of his sermons of a few years later could have been preached to any subsequent Catholic audience:

> Do not in any way doubt that this pilgrimage will not only earn you remission of sins and the reward of eternal life, but it will also offer much to wives, sons, parents, living or dead: whatever good you do in this life for them. This is the full and entire indulgence which the supreme pontiff, according to the keys committed to him by God, concedes to you.

Martyrs

In the same sermon James of Vitry stated the opinion of the Church's propagandists on the effect on the crusader of death in combat:

> Crusaders who, truly contrite and confessed, are girded in the service of God and then die in Christ's service are counted truly as martyrs, freed from both venial and mortal sins and from all enjoined penance, absolved from the penalties for sin in this world, from the penalties of purga-

tory in the next, secure from the torments of Gehenna, crowned with glory and honour in eternal beatitude.

A martyr does not, theoretically, need any indulgence, because the surrender of a life for love of God and neighbour has always been considered to be a sacrifice which immediately purges the individual concerned of all sinfulness. But the traditions of martyrdom related to heroic Christians who had passively accepted death for the faith and the conviction that those who died in a Holy War against the infidel were also martyrs, which was being expressed from the ninth century, was bound to be a subject of debate, since the internal dispositions of a man engaged in combat were not likely to be altruistic and serene. Nevertheless, the belief in warrior martyrs was taking hold in the eleventh century, being extended by Pope Leo IX to those who died simply in defence of justice, when he referred to the 'martyrdom' of those who had fallen in the defeat of his forces by the Normans in the battle of Civitate in 1053.

It became common for crusaders to be assured in sermons, tracts and chronicles that their death on campaign would be martyrdom. The prospect of immediate entry into paradise was held before them by propagandists like St Bernard:

Go forward then in security, knights, and drive off without fear the enemies of the Cross of Christ, certain that neither death nor life can separate you from the love of God which is in Jesus Christ . . . . How glorious are those who return victorious from the battle! How happy are those who die as martyrs in the battle! Rejoice, courageous athlete, if you survive and are victor in the Lord; but rejoice and glory the more if you die and are joined to the Lord. For your life is fruitful and your victory glorious. But death . . . is more fruitful and more glorious. For if those who die in the Lord are blessed, how much more so are those who die for the Lord!

It was one thing, however, for the Church to refer to martyrdom in its propaganda. It was quite another for it to state authoritatively that individuals, whose disposition at the moment of death was quite unknown, were now enjoying the beatific vision. Although the tombs of a few crusaders became cultic shrines, they were never officially recognized as saints because of their deaths in battle and were never commemorated in liturgical calendars; and in the early fourteenth century the old crusader John of Joinville forcefully expressed his disappointment that King Louis IX of France, who had died on crusade before Tunis in 1270, had been canonized not as a martyr but as a confessor. The Church was on safer ground with the guarantee of an indulgence, since the remission of sins assured by one was conditional on factors – true confession, contrition, altruism – over which it had no control and upon which it was not called to judge. Nevertheless the belief that dead crusaders were martyrs was so widespread that even senior churchmen had to pay lip service to it at times.

Privileges

The taking of the Cross had consequences for the status and rights of the man involved. He became, as we have seen, a temporary ecclesiastic, subject to the courts of the Church. The vow he had made was a means by which his immediate enthusiasm could be turned into a legal obligation, enforceable by the judges to whom he was now answerable, and as early as the First Crusade the papacy was prepared to excommunicate those who failed to carry out what they had promised. The Church courts would impose, or threaten to impose, the ecclesiastical sanctions of excommunication, interdict and suspension on reluctant crusaders, but men and women also gained the right to enjoy certain privileges as soon as they had taken the Cross or at least had begun to fulfil their obligations. All of them, apart from the indulgence and the right to benefit from the prayers offered for crusaders by the universal Church, which was not technically a privilege at all, were in fact exemptions from the operation of the law courts or invitations to the courts to act on a crusader's behalf. They can be divided into those which eased their lives in a world of legal niceties and technicalities and those which were descended from or were elaborations of the privileges enjoyed by earlier pilgrims.

One of the first group, the licence to clerics who joined the crusade to enjoy their benefices for a time, even though non-resident, and to pledge them to raise money for the journey, is to be found in the twelfth century, although it was not fully confirmed by the papacy until the thirteenth. The rest were granted from the pontificate of Innocent III onwards and by the middle of the thirteenth century may be summarized as: release from excommunication by virtue of taking the Cross; the licence to have dealings with excommunicates while on crusade without incurring censure; the right not to be cited for legal proceedings outside one's native diocese; freedom from the consequences of an interdict; the privilege of having a personal confessor, who was often allowed to dispense his patron from irregularities and to grant pardon for sins, like homicide, which were usually reserved for papal jurisdiction; and the right to count a crusade vow as an adequate substitute for another vow made previously but not yet carried out.

The privileges of the second group are more important. At the time of the First Crusade, pilgrims were subject in the same way as clerics to church courts; their persons were protected from attack; they were assured that lands and possessions seized by others during their absence would be returned to them; they could demand hospitality from the Church; they were in theory exempted from tolls and taxes and immune from arrest; and they may already have had the right to a suspension of legal proceedings in which they were involved until their return. Crusaders enjoyed the same rights from the first. As temporary churchmen they were subject in all but a few exceptional matters to ecclesiastical law and were exempt from most secular jurisdiction in cases that arose after they had taken the Cross. At Clermont Pope Urban accorded them the protection of the Truce of God and the papacy continued to stress that their persons should be secure. In their absence their families and properties were protected by the Church. Cases relating to this protection were already being examined by

ecclesiastical judges early in the twelfth century and the principles were stated at the First Lateran Council and in *Quantum
praedecessores*, to be constantly repeated thereafter:

> And we decree that their wives and children, goods and
> possessions should remain under the protection of Holy
> Church; under our protection and that of the archbishops,
> bishops and other prelates of the Church of God. And by
> apostolic authority we forbid any legal suit to be brought
> thereafter concerning any of the possessions they held
> peacefully when they took the Cross until there is absolutely
> certain knowledge of their return or death.

> Since [wrote Pope Gregory VIII to the crusader Hinco of
> Serotin in 1187] you...having assumed the sign of the
> living cross, propose to go to the aid of the Holy Land,
> we...take under the protection of St Peter and ourselves
> your person, with your dependants and those goods which
> you reasonably possess at present,...stating that they all
> should be kept undiminished and together from the time
> of your departure on pilgrimage overseas until your return
> or death is most certainly known.

The Church itself, through the agency of the bishops or,
with respect to some important crusaders, of special officials
called *conservatores crucesignatorum*, oversaw the protection of
the lands. It was common, particularly in England where the
crown often acted as the guardian of their property, for
crusaders also to appoint attorneys to defend their interests in
their absence. Crusaders also came to be entitled to *essoin*, a
delay in the performance of services and in judicial
proceedings to which they were a party until their return; to
a quick settlement of outstanding court cases if they so willed;
to permission to count the crusade as restitution of some article
stolen; to the right to dispose of or pledge fiefs or other
property which was ordinarily inalienable; to a moratorium
on debts and exemption from interest payments while on
crusade; and to freedom from tolls and taxes.

Who Were the Crusaders?

Two features of the vow were that it could be taken by anyone, of whatever sex or walk of life, and that the action promised was essentially temporary: a layman or a priest would put his normal occupation aside for a short time to go crusading. The appeal of the crusades was confined to no class. I have already referred to the large numbers of poor non-combatants attached to the early expeditions, who could not be prevented from joining because as pilgrimages crusades had to be open to all. The introduction of redemptions in the early thirteenth century eased the situation, because these men and women could now be encouraged to subscribe small sums of money in return for indulgences. More important still was the practice of carrying the armies to the East by sea: an overland march required of the poor only physical effort and their feet, whereas transportation by sea imposed on them the need to pay passage fees which few could afford. But the masses never left the stage entirely and in the fifteenth century, as the Turks advanced through the Balkans, armies of the poor were deliberately raised by famous crusade preachers like St John of Capistrano.

A significant part was also played by artisans, merchants, burgesses of all kinds, and even criminals, whose sentences could be commuted in return for taking part or settling in the Holy Land. In the late twelfth century, attempts were being made in England to list the crusaders living in certain districts: in Lincolnshire they were nearly all poor and included a clerk, a smith, a skinner, a potter, a butcher and a vintner; 43 crusaders were to be found in the archdeaconry of Cornwall, including a tailor, a smith, a shoemaker, two chaplains, a merchant, a miller, two tanners and two women. In 1250 the ship *St Victor*, bound for the East from France, was carrying 453 crusaders, of whom 14 were knights and leaders of groups, 90 retainers and seven clerics; the remaining 342 passengers were commoners and the surnames of several of them suggest burgess origins; 42 were women, 15 of whom accompanied their husbands, while one travelled with her father and two with their brothers.

69

Those taking part in a crusade could be travelling alone, although every knight would have had a few supporters, such as grooms and squires, with him. Magnates would be accompanied by their households, which could often be quite large: when the great nobleman Eudes of Burgundy, count of Nevers and lord of Bourbon, died in Palestine in July 1266 he was employing in his household four knights, three chaplains, seven squires, nine sergeants, 32 servants, five crossbowmen and four turcopoles. Cousins might travel together. So might knights or burgesses from the same district or town; the Italian towns of Asti and perhaps Siena chose commanders for their contingents. At the initiative of a local magnate or a high ecclesiastic, or town burgesses in the West, men might also organize themselves into a confraternity, a common form of religious association, though here committed to the defence of Christendom. As early as 1122 a confraternity in Spain was involved in the Reconquest and another in Toulouse was established by the bishop to take part in the Albigensian Crusade. Confraternities from Spain, Pisa, Lombardy and Tuscany, England and Châteaudun in France maintained bands of arms-bearers in the East, rather like the *milites ad terminum*, and their leaders played a significant part in the politics of the Kingdom of Jerusalem.

Unquestioned leadership over a crusading army was essential, but was rarely to be found. I have already pointed out that the pope's representatives were barred by canon law from becoming generals. When a king like Louis VII or Philip II or Richard I, or a very important magnate like Thibaut of Champagne or the Lord Edward of England took part, it was natural that he should be in command, but if two kings were on the same expedition they would never allow themselves to be subject to one another: the French troops on the Third Crusade remained obstinately independent of Richard of England even after the departure of Philip of France. It was quite common for groups of crusaders, thrown together by circumstances or drawn from the same region, to elect their own captains. Such men might be appointed temporarily – immediately after the arrival in Egypt of the first contingent

70

of the Fifth Crusade the crusaders chose someone to lead them until the rest of the army arrived — but full-time commanders were also elected. This procedure, which had been tried and had failed during the First Crusade, can be seen in operation during the planning for the Fourth Crusade, when Boniface of Montferrat was chosen as leader, and during the Fifth, for when they gathered for departure the crusaders from the Rhineland and the Low Countries elected William of Holland as captain and George of Wied as second-in-command. Once in Egypt the crusaders appear to have been divided into nations and the Germans seem to have chosen Adolf of Berg to lead them; after his death in 1218 George of Wied was elected to succeed him. It was, no doubt, essential for a noble to be chosen for such an office.

Without clear and unambiguous leadership every crusade was run by a committee made up of the great lords together with the legate. It was hard to get these often proud and touchy men to agree on any course of action, partly because they themselves could never make decisions independently of their own subordinates ·who were, like them, not conscripts or vassals performing feudal service, but volunteers. Unless the lesser nobles and knights were associated with the greater lords by ties of family or clientage back home, they were serving in the contingents of the magnates only because they expected provisions for their followers. They could easily transfer their loyalties to another lord or even abandon the crusade altogether if they thought they were not being properly led. All early crusades were characterized by a kaleidoscopic shifting of allegiances as minor lords moved from one contingent to another, or bodies of men and individuals came and went. Before any decisions binding on a whole army could be made, therefore, the great had to summon their own committees of followers to discuss them. One wonders how they were made at all. In the thirteenth century there were improvements in discipline, which stemmed from the decision of the papacy to raise large sums from the taxation of the Church, which were then allotted to those leaders who were taking the Cross. The system provided a way of subsidizing crusaders through their commanders and therefore of making them more dependent on them. But the independence which stemmed from the voluntary nature of the vow meant that nobles were never very amenable.

Crusaders drawn from so many walks of life must naturally have had many reasons for taking the Cross and their motives have been a subject for debate since the movement began. A popular generalization today is that they were attracted by the prospect of material gain, whether through colonization or booty. But although the First Crusade began the process by which Western Europeans conquered and settled many of the coastal territories of the eastern Mediterranean, it is very unlikely that this was planned from the start: most of the crusaders returned home once Jerusalem had fallen to them and colonists migrated to the region only after it had been conquered. With no proper system of provisioning, the early crusaders had to forage to survive, which explains their obsession with loot, but any plunder gained towards the end of the crusade would have been dissipated on the return journey, even supposing that men could have found the physical means to carry it home. Everyone agrees that material and ideological motivations are not mutually exclusive and it would be absurd to maintain that no one thought he could benefit in worldly terms – for one thing there were real advantages in enhanced prestige at home – but the profit motive, which has always rested on insufficient evidence, looks less and less convincing the more we know. An alternative, twentieth-century, explanation of the attraction of crusading is that families, growing larger and worried about the pressure on their lands, adopted strategies which encouraged or forced unwanted male members to seek their fortunes elsewhere and that crusading provided these supernumeraries with an outlet. But the reality was that far from being an economic safety-valve, crusading cost the families of volunteers much in financial terms. The only strategy for which there is evidence is one in which the kindred co-operated in damage limitation once a relation had taken the Cross. The costs of war to individuals planning to crusade were daunting and they rose inexorably as time progressed, which explains, as we have seen, the concern of the Church and secular rulers to provide crusaders with subsidies. Anyone who thought there was much to gain out of the crusades to the East would have been mad and while, of course, conditions in the Iberian peninsula and the Baltic region were different and some campaigners may well have been more interested in settlement, most in those regions, too, returned home after the expeditions. The last thing most sensible crusaders would have expected was material gain.

One cannot avoid concluding that crusading was a genuine devotional activity. This is made easier to understand once we accept that only a minority in each generation were moved to take the Cross. We do not have to suppose that everyone, or even most, found the movement in some way attractive, but we have to explain why some, who defined themselves by their commitment, did so. Many of the earliest crusaders, exposed for several decades to the intense evangelizing campaigns of the eleventh-century Church and obsessed by their sinfulness, appear to have responded to the penitential ethos. Convinced that their condition of existence left them with little hope of salvation, they were seizing an opportunity to better their chances in the afterlife. In the earliest period there is also evidence for concentrations of crusaders in certain noble families in which traditions of pilgrimage to Jerusalem, or attachment to the patronage of particular saints or to reformed monasticism, had generated a predisposition to respond to the appeal. Over time the practice generated its own traditions within kindreds, while local networks of attachment created by lordship were also having an influence on recruitment by the late thirteenth century. By the fourteenth, crusading had become one of the social obligations of chivalric culture, although it remained a penitential activity to the end. It is clear that men and women were deeply moved by the desire to serve Christ by taking up his Cross, defending the Church and physically occupying and holding the land sanctified by his presence.

Some Crusaders, Real and Imaginary

The Montlhéry Clan

By 1120 one family dominated the settlements in the Levant established by the First Crusade. King Baldwin II of Jerusalem had cousins everywhere. William of Bures-sur-Yvette and Hugh of Le Puiset were lords of Galilee and Jaffa, the two most strategically important seigneuries in his kingdom. Joscelin of Courtenay was count of Edessa in the north. The most important lordship in that county was held by Waleran of Le Puiset, whose brother was abbot of St Mary of the Valley of Jehoshaphat and custodian of the chief Marian shrine in Jerusalem, the tomb whence the Blessed Virgin Mary was believed to have been assumed into heaven.

These men were all descended from Guy I of Montlhéry in the Ile-de-France and his wife Hodierna of Gometz. Guy had been pious and, attracted to Cluniac monasticism, had founded the priory of Longpont-sous-Montlhéry, where he ended his days as a monk. Very typically, a streak of religiosity ran in the family alongside a tendency to extreme violence. Perhaps this explains why two of Guy and Hodierna's sons, the husbands of two of their daughters, six grandsons, a granddaughter and her husband, and the husband of another granddaughter, a great-grandson and the husband of a great-granddaughter took part in the First Crusade. This extraordinary record was due largely to the offspring of Guy and Hodierna's four daughters, the legendary Montlhéry sisters whose procreativity was mentioned with awe by the twelfth-century historian William of Tyre. They were married into the families of St Valéry and Le Puiset-Breteuil, which each sent three first crusaders, Bourcq of Rethel, which sent two, including Baldwin II himself, and Courtenay, which provided one. If one adds to this the contribution from the closely related families of Chaumont-en-Vexin, Broyes and Pont-Echanfray, two generations of this clan produced 26, perhaps 28, crusaders to and settlers in the East. They demonstrate how a kindred could respond almost en bloc to a summons which appealed to them.

Hugh of Chaumont-sur-Loire, Lord of Amboise

Hugh (*c*.1080–1129) was born into a family which had risen to prominence in the service of the counts of Anjou. He was the heir to one of the three towers of Amboise when he took the Cross in March 1096, at a ceremony at the abbey of Marmoutier near Tours presided over by the pope himself. Hugh had gone to Tours in the entourage of Count Fulk IV of Anjou and in his case a commitment to crusade may have been bound up with the resolution – temporary as it turned out – of a bitter dispute over his inheritance. This had originated in his belief that the count was setting up his cousin, Corba of Thorigné, as a co-heiress of Amboise with the complicity of his uncle Lisois, who had had wardship of his estate in his minority. Part of the plan had been to marry Corba off to a man called Aimery of Courron. Hugh, who was only about 16 years old, had reacted fiercely, but the count had intervened and the quarrel had been patched up. Hugh and Aimery, who had also taken the Cross, left for the East together. Hugh had helped finance his crusade by pledging his lordship to a cousin on his mother's side called Robert of Roches-Corbon, to whom he had entrusted the custody of his castle. He had also been given a large sum of money for the crusade by his maternal uncle. In eleventh-century French society maternal uncles were the natural protectors of their sisters' children. Paternal uncles, like Lisois, were natural competitors for the patrimony.

During the three-year campaign Hugh gained a reputation for steadiness. He was one of those deputed to guard the gates of the city of Antioch against break-out as disintegration threatened the army on the night of 10 June 1098, when crusaders, desperate to get away and on the road home, were escaping even through the latrine-drains in the city walls. He took part in the gruesome siege of Ma'arrat late in 1098 and in the capture of Jerusalem in July 1099, and he fought in the final victory over the Egyptians in the battle of Ascalon a month later. He then fulfilled his vow at the Holy Sepulchre and began his journey home.

Around 1100 the Church's advice to returning crusaders was that 'now their robes had been washed clean' they should avoid muddying them again by withdrawing from the world and entering the religious life. But for a head of family, which had already made material sacrifices to help finance him, such a step would have been grossly irresponsible. For many crusaders their return marked a re-entry into a disfunctional society with which they had again to come to terms and which seems often to have become more disordered because of their absence. Hugh was one of those who found themselves forced to resort to violence. Aimery of Courron had been mortally wounded before the city of Nicaea in the summer of 1097 and the news of his death had been brought back to Anjou by fugitives from Antioch. Returning to the count's court at Loches at Easter 1100 'somewhat weighed down by illness', Hugh discovered that in his absence Count Fulk had been bribed to marry Corba to an elderly man called Achard of Saintes without taking advice from Corba's mother or informing Robert of Roches-Corbon. This meant that there was a new threat to Hugh's possession of his lordship. Achard, who knew well what the consequences of Hugh's arrival would be, fled with his young wife to Tours, but he was followed by Hugh's subjects, one of whom made contact with Corba and planned her abduction when she went to pray in a church nearby. One day she was bundled out of the church and on to a horse, and was handed over to a party of her kinsmen, led by Robert of Roches-Corbon. Achard died of illness and sorrow soon afterwards. Corba herself, with a new husband, took the Cross for (and died on) the third wave of the crusade in 1101, perhaps because she felt that Aimery of Courron's vow had not been fulfilled.

Hugh was unusual for the time in that he crusaded twice. In 1129, nearly three decades after he had come back from Jerusalem, he sailed to the East with his brother-in-law, Count Fulk V of Anjou, who was to marry Baldwin II's daughter and inherit the crown of Jerusalem. Now hugely rich and in possession of the rest of the seigneurie of Amboise, Hugh had made over his lordship to his eldest son. He obviously wanted to end his days in Jerusalem and it was there that he died two months after reaching Palestine. He was buried on the Mount of Olives, from where he would have looked down on the city 30 years before.

Leopold VI, Duke of Austria

Multiple crusading was becoming much more common in the late twelfth century and few were more enthusiastic than Leopold of Austria (1176/7–1230). He came from a crusading family. His father had quarrelled violently with Richard I of England during the Third Crusade and had arrested the king when on his return to the West he tried to slip through his territories in disguise. Leopold took the Cross in 1208 and took it again for the Fifth Crusade, in which he served from 1217 to 1219. In 1212 he also fought against the Cathars in the Albigensian Crusade, before going on from Languedoc to Spain take part in the Castilian crusade against the Moors. It has been suggested that his absences on crusade may have been motivated more by politics than ideology, but it is hard to see why he should have felt the need to make himself scarce, since the part he had played in the tortuous affairs of Germany had been conciliatory and sensible. He looks far more like one of those zealots who were often to be found in the thirteenth century. If so, it was characteristic of Pope Innocent III that he should try to cut him down to size:

> There is much more merit in the gibbet of Christ's cross than in the little sign of yours ... For you accept a soft and gentle cross; he suffered one that was bitter and hard. You bear it superficially on your clothing; he endured his in the reality of his flesh. You sew yours on with linen or silk threads; he was fastened to his with hard, iron nails.

Geoffrey of Sergines

Geoffrey (c.1205–69) came from a village north of Sens and not far from Paris. His family had close links with the Church:

a brother was abbot of St Jacques-de-Provins; Peter of Sergines, the archbishop of Tyre, who was captured by the Muslims at the battle of La Forbie in 1244, may have been a relation; and so may have been Margaret of Sergines who was abbess of Montivilliers. Geoffrey's son, also called Geoffrey, was in the East in the 1260s, served with Charles of Anjou in southern Italy and died on Louis IX's second crusade in 1270.

Geoffrey is mentioned in connection with military engagements in Palestine in 1242 and 1244 and the most likely date for his arrival in the East would be 1 September 1239, with a crusade under Count Thibaut of Champagne and Duke Hugh of Burgundy. He returned to France in 1244 and in 1248 travelled East with King Louis IX, to whom he had been closely attached as early as 1236. In his account of Louis's crusade in Egypt John of Joinville wrote of Geoffrey as one who, like himself, was among the king's closest confidants. He was one of a select band of eight companions who stood guard over the king at Damietta and throughout the crusade he was to be found in the king's council and entrusted with important duties. On 5 April 1250, as the crusade retired in disorder from Mansurah, he alone stood by and protected the king. Louis was later to say that Geoffrey had defended him against the Egyptians as a good valet swats the flies around his lord. Before he set out for home in April 1254 Louis arranged to leave Geoffrey behind in Acre as seneschal of the kingdom of Jerusalem and captain of a contingent of 100 knights financed by himself, with money to employ additional crossbowmen and sergeants.

The seneschalcy was the most prestigious and demanding of the great offices of the crown of Jerusalem and Geoffrey was to hold it until his death. In the absence of the king or regent, and provided the ruler had not appointed a lieutenant to represent him, the seneschal presided over meetings of the High Court, the most important of the royal courts in which all liege-vassals of the crown had the right to sit and speak. He was, therefore, *ex officio* the second man in the judicial hierarchy. He also supervised the *secrete*, the royal financial office and treasury, which worked according to Muslim methods. Geoffrey's long period of office must have given him an unrivalled experience of the working of the courts and royal administration. From 1259 to September 1261 and from 1264 to 1267 he governed Palestine on behalf of absent regents and from September 1261 to 1263, and perhaps for a few months in 1264, he was regent himself. With only a few breaks, therefore, he ruled the kingdom of Jerusalem from 1259 to 1267 and he did so well; alone of the governors of the period his reputation for severe though impartial justice was recognized by contemporaries.

He returned briefly to the West in the early 1260s. At this time he took the Cross once more and planned to travel East with a large company of knights. On 13 February 1262 Pope Urban IV gave him licence, as a crusader, to have a portable altar at which Mass could be celebrated; his chaplain was permitted to administer the sacraments to his knights and companions, and he was exempted from any decree of excommunication or interdict unless he was specifically named in a papal decree. The next few years revealed his devotion to the crusading cause, which was to keep him in the East until his death on 11 April 1269 and which nearly bankrupted him. In spite of assistance from the French crown and from the papacy there are many references to the financial straits in which he found himself; in 1267 he was threatening to sell his patrimony in France if he was not helped.

His qualities were conventional – John of Joinville referred to him as a 'good knight and prud'homme' – and they were summed up in a remarkable poem, *La complainte de Monseigneur Geoffrei de Sergines*, written in 1255–6 by the French poet Rutebeuf, who knew the region from which he came. To Rutebeuf Geoffrey was the finest of all knights: loyal, valiant and bounteous of soul. When he lived in France he was known as a gentle, courteous and debonair man with much love for God and Holy Church. He never deceived anyone, feeble or strong, and he was generous to poor neighbours:

> He loved his liege-lord so much
> That he went with him to avenge

> The shame of God over the seas.
> One ought to love such a prud'homme.
> With the king he moved and went,
> With the king he there remained
> With the king he bore good and ill.
> There has never been such a man.

Geoffrey was very pious, which would explain why he got on so well with Louis. The popes of the 1260s wrote of him as one who was totally committed to crusading, to the extent of exercising a ministry: 'devoting himself wholly in the ministry for the Crucified One . . . the one and only minister in the defence of the Holy Land'. He was not only a crusader, of course. His career, and those of several contemporaries, marked the high point of the tradition of the *milites ad terminum*, the knights who out of devotion offered their services to the defence of the Holy Land.

Chaucer's knight

Multiple crusading was so common a feature of the fourteenth century that it was caricatured by Geoffrey Chaucer in his portrait of the knight on the Canterbury pilgrimage:

> Full worthy was he in his lordes werre,
> And therto had he riden, no man ferre,
> As wel in cristendom as in hethenesse,
> And evere honoured for his worthynesse.
> At Alisaundre he was when it was wonne.
> Ful ofte tyme he hadde the bord bigonne
> Above alle nacions in Pruce;
> In Lettow hadde he reysed and in Ruce,
> No Cristen man so ofte of his degree.
> In Gernade at the seege eek hadde he be
> Of Algezir, and riden in Belmarye.
> At Lyeys was he and at Satalye,
> Whan they were wonne; and in the Grete See
> At many a noble armee hadde he be.

Engaged in 'his lordes werre' (the war of Christ or the crusade), the knight had fought in all the main theatres: the Baltic region, the Iberian peninsula and the eastern Mediterranean. He had joined the many knights from all over Europe who travelled to Prussia, Livonia (Lettow) and Russia in the north to take part in the *Reysen* of the Teutonic Knights, who had gained from the papacy the right to issue crusade indulgences. The *Reysen* were winter and summer raids into pagan Lithuania and Orthodox Russia and those who joined could leave shields painted with their coats-of-arms hanging in the fortresses of Marienburg or Königsberg. After a *Reysa* a feast would sometimes be held, with a table of honour for those who had most distinguished themselves by their prowess. In 1375 the grand master Winrich of Kniprode, who exploited chivalric theatre more than any other, presented each of the 12 knights at the table of honour with a shoulder badge on which was written in gold letters *Honneur vainc tout*. Chaucer must have imagined his knight sitting among these paladins, because he 'hadde the bord bigonne' in Prussia, presumably at the great headquarters castle of Marienburg.

The knight had taken part in the crusade, joined by nobles from all over Europe, including the earls of Derby and Salisbury, which had invaded the Moorish kingdom of Granada and had taken Algeçiras after a two-year siege (1342–4), thereby blocking the Strait of Gibraltar and preventing the arrival of large numbers of Muslim reinforcements from Africa. He had raided into Morocco (Belmarye). He had been in the force of King Peter of Cyprus which had taken Antalya (Satalye) in southern Asia Minor in 1361. He had also fought in Peter's crusade which occupied Alexandria for a few days in October 1365 and had raided Ayas (Lyeys) in Cilicia in 1367.

Chaucer's picture may have been a caricature, but it was not untypical. Henry Grosmont, duke of Lancaster, was reported to have crusaded to Granada, Prussia, Rhodes and Cyprus. John Boucicaut, the marshal of France, went four times on Prussian *Reysen* and took the Cross for King Peter's crusade to Alexandria and again for the crusade to Mahdia in North Africa in 1390, although the king of France forbade him to go; he went back to Prussia instead. He was on the Balkan crusade of Nicopolis in 1396 and ran his own crusade in the eastern Mediterranean region around 1400. The enthusiasm of European nobles for crusading as a chivalric as well as a religious exercise – at a time when many of them were also involved in the Hundred Years War – explains why there was barely a year in the fourteenth century when there was not a crusade in action somewhere on the Christian frontiers.

The Military Orders

It is questionable whether one ought to consider the brothers of the military orders at all in a chapter on crusaders. It is true that the military orders were founded as, or developed into, institutions closely associated with the crusading movement and inspired by its ideals, and it was because of this that some of them became very well endowed. They were committed to the reconquest of Christian territory and the defence of Christendom and they operated alongside crusaders or in the same regions as they did. They were associated with the movement by its apologists, particularly St Bernard who, in his defence of the Templars, the *De laude novae militae*, developed with reference to them the theme of the new knighthood fighting on behalf of Christ. Some eight decades later, James of Vitry defined their duties very much in terms of the crusades:

> The brothers of the military orders are ordained to defend Christ's church with the material sword, especially against those who are outside it; that is against the Muslims in Syria, against the Moors in Spain, against the pagans in Prussia, Livonia and Comania . . . against schismatics in Greece and against heretics everywhere dispersed throughout the universal church.

The orders, he went on, differed in their habits and customs, 'but all are united in defence of the Church against infidels'.

And in the middle of the thirteenth century St Thomas Aquinas drew attention to their association with penitential violence when he justified their role by pointing out that: 'To make war in the service of God is imposed on some as a penance, as is evident from those who are enjoined to fight in aid of the Holy Land.'

But the fact remained that the brothers were not crusaders. Some, like the Templars, took vows which, at least in the actions to be performed – the reconquest of Jerusalem and the defence of the Holy Land – had similarities to those of crusaders, but others did not. The promises made by a brother of the Hospital of St John – to be obedient and chaste, to live in poverty as a serf and slave of the sick – made no reference whatever to the defence of Christendom. And even when a military order did impose a vow upon its members to defend Christendom, the form the promise took made it fundamentally different from that of a crusader. The brother of a military order was permanently committed to his duty; he was not a pilgrim, whose condition was essentially temporary, and so the concept of pilgrimage did not enter into his vow at all. The distinction was stressed in one of James of Vitry's sermons, in which he told the story of a crusader who had been captured along with some Templars by the Muslims. On being asked if he was a Templar he replied, 'I am a secular knight and a pilgrim.'

It is not easy to generalize about the military orders because there were many of them and among them there was great variation. They followed different rules. Some, like the Orders of the Temple, the Hospital of St John and St Lazarus, drew recruits from all parts of Latin Christendom; others, like the Orders of St Mary of the Germans (the Order of the Teutonic Knights and often called the Teutonic Order), Santiago, Alcantara, Calatrava, Christ, Montesa and St Thomas, were nationally based. Some, like the Temple and the Hospital, were immensely rich; others were tiny and poor. Some were prototypes of the great international orders that grew up in the later Middle Ages, being highly privileged, exempt from the authority of diocesan bishops and answerable only to Rome; others were in terms of privilege quite insignificant.

Two, St Mary of the Germans and the Hospital, were to establish quasi-sovereign order-states in Prussia, Rhodes and Malta. The whole *raison d'être* of some was the defence of the faith; but others, like the Hospital of St John, had originated as purely charitable institutions which had only slowly, and then with the disapproval of the popes, turned themselves into military orders, and in them charitable activities remained a primary responsibility. Others still, like St Mary of the Germans, were founded both to fight and to care for the sick.

Nevertheless, there were some important and fundamental similarities. All were religious orders, for which solemn vows were made and in which the brothers followed rules of life and the monastic *horarium* and submitted themselves to canonical discipline. Their essential characteristic was that a number of the professed lay brothers were themselves warriors. Any religious institution could have vassals owing military services or could employ mercenaries to garrison castles and protect territory, but these would not make it a military order. The military orders themselves made use of vassals and many mercenaries – in any engagement the number of brothers-at-arms in their forces was comparatively small – but it was the class of fighting brothers that gave them their special features. And it was these lay brothers (rather than the priests as was normal in most religious orders), who came to dominate them, being far more numerous and providing the great and lesser officers.

They never had any difficulty in drawing in recruits, even as late as the eighteenth century, although their wealth, privileges and rivalries and a suspicion (very general in the West and rather unfair) that they were not pulling their weight made them increasingly unpopular with the clergy and with ordinary people in the thirteenth century. Internationally run and highly privileged instruments of papal power, echoing contemporary notions of ecclesiastical administration, the structures of the greater among them proved inadequate for their needs, even if their estate management was often quite efficient at a regional level. This led to the paradox that, although the spearheads of what were among the richest religious orders of the time, the headquarters convents in Palestine were always starved of money and often near bankruptcy. The brothers in the East, standing to arms in a defensive war, marooned themselves in those magnificent fortresses which today still stand as mute monuments to the ideal of the just cause, the most beautiful and most depressing reminders of it. Yet, by one of those quirks of history, two of the orders, the Hospital of St John of Jerusalem and St Mary of the Germans, have survived. Both, especially the Hospital of St John on Rhodes until 1523 and on Malta until 1798, have played an important role into modern times, and although today their tasks have greatly changed they are living relics of the age of the crusades.

5 *When Were the Crusades?*

We are now coming to the end of our enquiry and have reached the stage at which we can make a definition. A crusade was a penitential war which ranked as, and had many of the attributes of, a pilgrimage. It manifested itself in many theatres of war: Palestine and the eastern Mediterranean region, of course, but also North Africa, Spain, the Baltic shores, Poland, Hungary, the Balkans and even Western Europe. The Muslims provided the opposition in North Africa and Spain as well as in Palestine and Syria, and, from the fourteenth century onwards, in the Aegean and the Balkans; but crusaders were also engaged in campaigns against Pagan Wends, Balts and Lithuanians, Shamanist Mongols, Orthodox Russians and Greeks, Cathar and Hussite heretics and Catholic political opponents of the papacy. The cause – the recovery of property or defence against injury – was just in the traditional sense, but it was related to the needs of all Christendom or the Church, rather than to those of a particular nation or region. A crusade was legitimized by the pope as head of Christendom and representative of Christ, rather than by a temporal ruler, and being Christ's own enterprise it was positively holy. At least some of the participants took a vow, which subordinated them to the Church and ensured some papal control over them in matters other than the actual waging of war. Pilgrimage terminology was often used of them; and some of the privileges they enjoyed, particularly the protection of themselves, their families and properties, were associated with those of pilgrims. They believed themselves to be penitents and as such they were granted a full remission of sins, which after 1198 was reformulated as a plenary indulgence. When they were not engaged in war in the East, the remission of sins or indulgence was related to those given to crusaders in the Holy Land.

One ought now to try to give chronological bounds to the movement. When was the first and when the last crusade? In 1074 Pope Gregory VII was planning a campaign in the East. The Seljuk Turks were overrunning Asia Minor and the young Byzantine emperor Michael VII, disregarding the bad feelings between the Latin and Greek Churches, had appealed to the new pope for aid. Gregory, who was hoping to bring the Churches together, reacted positively and there survive five letters written by him to various correspondents between February and December. He dwelt on the sufferings of the Eastern Christians and the necessity of bringing them fraternal aid. He compared service in the army to service of the Church, calling on one man 'to defend the Christian faith and the heavenly king' and exclaiming that while it was glorious to die for one's fatherland it was still more glorious to die for Christ. He stressed the spiritual rewards that would result, writing that 'through the work of a moment you can acquire eternal mercy'. The expedition was his own and he might lead it himself. He reported to King Henry IV of Germany that over 50,000 men were ready to go if they would have the pope 'in the expedition as leader and high priest', and he even suggested that under him the army might push on to the Holy Sepulchre. He was thinking, extraordinarily enough, of leaving Henry behind to defend the Roman Church in his absence. Much of this, of course, was hyperbole and the plans were overtaken by the Investiture Controversy. But one can identify in Gregory's letters the concept of a Holy War and papal authorization of it, eternal reward and above all a reference to Jerusalem. Gregory's ideas may have been more developed than these letters reveal. We know that he introduced the notion of penitential war a few years later and that he was regarded in the papal circle as the father of the crusades, while it is likely that Pope Urban II saw himself following in the footsteps of his master. But on the evidence before us we cannot go so far. Gregory's letters contain no clear association between the planned expedition and a pilgrimage, no reference to fighting for the remission of sins and no sign of the vow and the consequent protection for the soldiers. Until further evidence comes to light, one is forced to conclude that the plans of 1074 were not really those for a crusade, that the traditional date of 1095 for the origins of the crusading movement is correct and that it stemmed from an initiative taken by Urban II.

It may be said to have ended definitively when the Knights Hospitallers of St John, the last members of a military order ruling an order-state still engaged in naval warfare against Muslims, surrendered Malta to Napoleon Bonaparte on 13 June 1798. By then many of the elements of crusading had already withered away. The last crusades answering to the definition I have given had probably been the expedition of Sebastian of Portugal to Morocco in 1578 and the Spanish Armada to England ten years later. Although crusading in the seventeenth century still awaits intensive study, the last crusade league had been the Holy League, from 1684 to 1697, which recovered the Peloponnese for a time. There may have been men who had taken the Cross in the early eighteenth century, fighting in the armies of Venice or Austria against the Turks, but the nearer we get to the present day the more the mists swirl in, obscuring our vision. Research on the last period of crusading is very badly needed. Until it is done, the story of the decline of that extraordinary and durable movement cannot be satisfactorily told.

Chronology

1095	March	The Council of Piacenza
	July (–September 1096)	Pope Urban II's preaching journey
	27 November	Proclamation of the crusade at the Council of Clermont
	December (–July 1096)	Persecution of Jews in France, Germany and Bohemia
1096–1102		**The First Crusade**
1099	15 July	Jerusalem falls to the crusaders
1103		Planned crusade of Emperor Henry IV
1107–8		Crusade of Bohemond of Antioch-Taranto
1108–9		Crusade of Bertrand of St Gilles
1114		Catalan Crusade to Balearic Islands
1120–26		Crusade of Pope Calixtus II in the East and in Spain
1120		Foundation of the Knights Templar
1126		First evidence for the militarization of the Hospital of St John
1128–9		Crusade to the East of King Baldwin II of Jerusalem

1139–40		Crusade to the East
1145		Pope Eugenius III's crusade proclamation *Quantum praedecessores*
1146		Persecution of Jews in the Rhineland
1146–7		St Bernard preaches the crusade
1147	13 April	Pope Eugenius III authorizes crusading in Spain and beyond the north-eastern frontier of Germany
1147–9		**The Second Crusade**
1147	24 October	Capture of Lisbon
1153		Crusade in Spain
1157–84		Several papal calls to crusade, answered by some small and medium-sized expeditions to the East
1157–8		Crusade in Spain
1171		Crusade in the Baltic region
1175		Crusade in Spain
1177		Crusade to the East of Philip of Flanders
1187	4 July	The army of the Kingdom of Jerusalem annihilated by Saladin in the Battle of Hattin
	2 October	Jerusalem taken by Saladin
	29 October	Pope Gregory VIII's crusade proclamation *Audita tremendi*
1188	January	Imposition of the Saladin Tithe in England
1189–92		**The Third Crusade**
1190		Persecution of Jews in England
1191	June	Richard I of England occupies Cyprus

1193–1230		The Livonian Crusade (to modern Latvia)
1193		Crusade in Spain
1197–8		German crusade to the East
1198		Foundation of the Teutonic Order
	August	Pope Innocent III's crusade proclamation *Post miserabile*
1199	24 November	Pope Innocent III proclaims a crusade in Italy against Markward of Anweiler
	December	Institution of the taxation of the Church for crusaders
1202–4		**The Fourth Crusade**
1204		Pope Innocent III allows recruitment for the Livonian Crusade on a regular basis
	12–15 April	Sack of Constantinople by the crusaders
1206		Danish crusade to Ösel
1208	14 January	Assassination of Peter of Castelnau, the papal legate in Languedoc
		Pope Innocent III proclaims the Albigensian Crusade
1209–29		The Albigensian Crusade
1212		The Children's Crusade
		Crusade in Spain
1213	April	Pope Innocent III's crusade proclamation *Quia major*
1215	November	The Fourth Lateran Council permits regular taxation of the Church for crusading and issues the crusade constitution *Ad Liberandam*
1216	28 October	King Henry III of England takes the Cross against English rebels

1217–29		**The Fifth Crusade**
1219		Danish crusade to Estonia
1225		The Teutonic Order invited to Prussia
1227		Crusade against heretics in Bosnia authorized (renewed in 1234)
1228–9		Crusade to the East of Emperor Frederick II
1229		The Teutonic Order begins the conquest of Prussia
	18 February	Jerusalem restored to the Christians by treaty
1229–53		Crusade in Spain, involving James I of Aragon and Ferdinand III of Castile
1231		Crusade of John of Brienne in aid of Constantinople
1232–4		Crusade against the Stedinger heretics in Germany
1239–40		Crusade in aid of Constantinople
1239–41		**Crusade to the East of Thibaut of Champagne and Richard of Cornwall**
1239		Proclamation of a crusade against Emperor Frederick II (renewed 1240, 1244)
		Swedish crusade to Finland
1241		Proclamation of a crusade against the Mongols (renewed 1243, 1249)
1244	11 July–23 August	Jerusalem lost to the Muslims
1245		The Teutonic Order allowed to wage a permanent crusade in Prussia

1248–54	**The First Crusade to the East of St Louis (King Louis IX of France)**
1248	Crusade against Emperor Frederick II in Germany
1251	The First Crusade of the Shepherds
1254	Crusade to Prussia
1255	Crusades preached in Italy against the opponents of the papacy
1261 25 July	The Greeks reoccupy Constantinople
1265–6	Crusade of Charles of Anjou to southern Italy
1269–72	**The Second Crusade of St Louis**
1269	Aragonese crusade to the East
1271–2	English crusade under the Lord Edward in the East
1274 18 May	The Second Council of Lyons issues the crusade decree *Constitutiones pro zelo fidei*
1283–1302	Crusade against the Sicilians and Aragonese
1287	Crusade to the East of Alice of Blois
1288	Crusade to the East of John of Grailly
1290	Crusades to the East of Otto of Grandson and the North Italians
1291 18 May	The port-city of Acre falls to the Muslims; the last Christian strongholds on the mainland evacuated by August
1306–1522	Hospitaller rule over the island of Rhodes

1306–7		Crusade against the followers of Fra Dolcino in Piedmont
1307		Crusade proclaimed in support of Charles of Valois's claims to Constantinople
	13 October	Arrest of all the Templars in France
1309		The Popular Crusade
		The Teutonic Order moves its headquarters to Prussia
1309–10		Castilian and Aragonese crusade in Spain
		Crusade against Venice
1310		Hospitaller crusade to Rhodes
1312	3 April	The Order of the Knights Templar suppressed
1314		Crusade in Hungary against Mongols and Lithuanians (renewed 1325, 1332, 1335, 1352, 1354)
1320		The Second Crusade of the Shepherds
1321		Crusade in Italy against the opponents of the papacy (extended 1324)
1323		Norwegian crusade against the Russians in Finland
1325		Crusade in Poland against Mongols and Lithuanians (renewed 1340, 1343, 1351, 1354, 1355, 1363, 1369)
1328		Crusade proclaimed against King Louis IV of Germany
		Crusade in Spain
1332–4		First Crusade League to the eastern Mediterranean

1340	Crusade against heretics in Bohemia
30 October	Crusading victory in the Battle of Salado (Spain)
1342–4	Crusaders besiege Algeçiras (Spain)
1344	Crusade to the Canary Islands planned
28 October	Crusade League to the eastern Mediterranean occupies Smyrna
1345–7	Crusade to the East of Humbert, dauphin of Viennois
1345	Genoese crusade to defend Kaffa against the Mongols
1348	Crusade of King Magnus of Sweden to Finland (renewed 1350, 1351)
1349–50	Crusaders besiege Gibraltar
1353–7	Crusade to regain control of the Papal State in Italy
1359	Crusade League in the eastern Mediterranean
1360	Crusade against Milan (renewed 1363, 1368)
1365–7	Crusade of King Peter I of Cyprus in the East
1366	Crusade of Amadeus of Savoy to the Dardanelles and Bulgaria
1383	Crusade of the bishop of Norwich against the Clementists in Flanders
1386	Crusade of John of Gaunt in Castile
1390	Crusade to Mahdia in North Africa
1396	Crusade of Nicopolis (defeated by the Turks, 25 September)

1398		Proclamation of a crusade to defend Constantinople (renewed 1399, 1400)
1399–1403		Crusade of John Boucicaut in the eastern Mediterranean
1420–31		The Hussite Crusades
1444		Crusade of Varna (defeated by the Turks, 19 November)
1453	29 May	Constantinople falls to the Turks
	30 September	Proclamation of a new crusade to the East
1455		Genoese crusade in defence of Chios
1456		Crusade of St John of Capistrano (successful defence of Belgrade against the Turks, 22 July)
1460	14 January	Proclamation of the crusade of Pope Pius II
1464	15 August	Pope Pius II dies while waiting for his crusade to muster at Ancona
1471	31 December	Crusade to the East proclaimed
1472		Crusade League in the eastern Mediterranean
1481		Crusade to recover Otranto from the Turks
1482–92		Crusade in Spain
1492	2 January	Granada falls to the crusaders
1493		Crusade in Hungary against the Turks
1499–1510		Spanish Crusade establishes beachheads on the North African coast
1500	1 June	Proclamation of a crusade against the Turks

1513		Crusade proclaimed in Eastern Europe against the Turks
1517	11 November	Proclamation of a crusade against the Turks
1522	July–18 December	Turkish siege of Rhodes, ending in surrender of Rhodes by the Hospitallers of St John
1529	26 September–October	First Ottoman siege of Vienna
1530–1798		Hospitaller rule over the Island of Malta
1530	2 February	Proclamation of a crusade against the Turks
1535		Crusade of Emperor Charles V to Tunis
1537–8		Crusade League in the eastern Mediterranean
1541		Crusade of Emperor Charles V to Algiers
1550		Crusade of Emperor Charles V to Mahdia
1560		Crusade of King Philip II of Spain to Jerba and Tripoli
1565	19 May–8 September	Unsuccessful siege of Malta by the Turks
1570–3		Holy (Crusade) League operating in the Mediterranean
1570–1		Fall of Cyprus to the Turks
1571	7 October	Naval victory of the League under Don John of Austria in the Battle of Lepanto
1573	11 October	Tunis temporarily occupied by Don John of Austria
1578		Crusade of King Sebastian of Portugal to Morocco
1588		The Armada (a crusade against England)

1645–69		Crete invaded and conquered by the Turks. Defended by a crusade league
1683	14 July – 12 September	Second Ottoman siege of Vienna
1684–97		Holy (Crusade) League begins the recovery of the Balkans
1798	13 June	Malta surrenders to Napoleon

Select Bibliography of Secondary Works

H. E. Mayer, in his *Bibliographie zur Geschichte der Kreuzzüge* (Hanover, 1960), compiled a first-class bibliography of books and articles published before 1958–9, containing over 5,000 titles. He issued supplements for the years 1958–67 as 'Literaturbericht über die Geschichte der Kreuzzüge', *Historische Zeitschrift*, Sonderheft III (1969) and for the years 1967–82, with J. McLellan, in a 'Select Bibliography of the Crusades', in K. M. Setton (editor-in-chief), *A History of the Crusades*, vol. 6 (see below). His regular short reviews for *Deutsches Archiv für Erforschung des Mittelalters* are worth consulting. The lists of recent publications and the accounts of work in progress in the *Bulletin of the Society for the Study of the Crusades and the Latin East* are a good guide to what is being brought out year by year. The Society is now planning to publish a journal, entitled *Crusades*.

The best treatment of historiography has been written by G. Constable, 'The Historiography of the Crusades', *The Crusades from the Perspective of Byzantium and the Muslim World*, ed. A. E. Laiou and R. P. Mottahedeh (Washington, DC, 2001). When dealing with the controversy about definition, Constable places the partisans in four categories. The comments that follow are mine.

1. **Generalists** Their best representative was C. Erdmann, *The Origin of the Idea of the Crusade* (1935; English trans. Princeton, 1977). A modern follower is E.-D. Hehl, 'Was ist eigentlich ein Kreuzzug', *Historische Zeitschrift* 259 (1994). Perhaps to be put in this group, although in some ways his approach is closer to Nietzschean relativism, is C. J. Tyerman, who expanded his article 'Were there any Crusades in the Twelfth Century?', *English Historical Review* 110 (1995) into a book, *The Invention of*

the Crusades (Basingstoke, 1998), which is not intellectually rigorous enough to be convincing.

2. **Popularists** A good example is P. Alphandéry and A. Dupront, *La Chrétienté et l'idée de croisade*, 2 vols (Paris, 1954–9). Their modern protagonist is J. Flori in *Pierre l'Ermite et la Première Croisade* (Paris, 1999) and *La guerre sainte: La formation de l'idée de croisade dans l'Occident chrétien* (Paris, 2001).

3. **Traditionalists** The leader today is H. E. Mayer in *The Crusades* (2nd edn, Oxford, 1988 – but see especially the 1st English edn, Oxford, 1972). He is supported, if indirectly, by J. Richard in *The Crusades, c.1071–c.1291* (1996, English trans. Cambridge, 1999), who accepts the pluralist position, but then argues that crusades to the East were characterized by 'a visceral attachment to the Holy Land', which gives them their own particular ethos.

4. **Pluralists** The present book and several others written by myself and by N. J. Housley, E. Siberry and C. T. Maier (see below) are considered to be pluralist. So is the brief history of B. Hamilton, *The Crusades* (Stroud, 1998). A clear and articulate defence of the position is by N. J. Housley in *The Later Crusades, 1274–1580: From Lyons to Alcazar* (Oxford, 1992). A colourful example of pluralism in practice is J. S. C. Riley-Smith (ed.), *The Atlas of the Crusades* (London, 1991).

Relatively up-to-date short histories of the crusades are H. E. Mayer, *The Crusades* (see above), which treats the crusades to the East before 1291, and J. S. C. Riley-Smith, *The Crusades: A Short History* (London, 1987), which also covers the other theatres of war and takes the story to the eighteenth century. A thematic treatment of the subject can be found in J. S. C. Riley-Smith (ed.), *The Oxford Illustrated History of the Crusades* (Oxford, 1995). Of the large-scale works, R. Grousset, *Histoire des croisades et du royaume franc de Jérusalem*, 3 vols (Paris, 1934–6) and S. Runciman, *A History of the Crusades*, 3 vols (Cambridge, 1951–4) are now very dated, and K. M. Setton (editor-in-chief), *A History of the Crusades*, 6 vols (2nd edn, Madison, 1969–89) suffers from the usual failings of collaborative projects, although some individual chapters are good and others are on topics not easily read about elsewhere. Much new material on the later crusades was revealed by K. M. Setton, *The Papacy and the Levant (1204–1571)*, 4 vols (Philadelphia, 1976–84). The best treatment of them is by N. J. Housley, *The Later Crusades, 1274–1580* (see above). Housley has also written a good book on the fourteenth century: *The Avignon Papacy and the Crusades, 1305–1378* (Oxford, 1986).

Surveys of crusading thought have generally fallen into two categories. First, there are those which base their approach on canon law: M. Villey, *La croisade: essai sur la formation d'une théorie juridique* (Paris, 1942); J. A. Brundage, *Medieval Canon Law and the Crusader* (Madison, 1969); F. H. Russell, *The Just War in the Middle Ages* (Cambridge, 1975); M. Purcell, *Papal Crusading Policy, 1244–1291* (Leiden, 1975); J. Muldoon, *Popes, Lawyers and Infidels* (Liverpool, 1979). See also J. Brundage, 'The Crusader's Wife: A Canonistic Quandary', *Studia Gratiana* 12 (1967) and 'The Crusader's Wife Revisited', *Studia Gratiana* 14 (1967); R. H. Schmandt, 'The Fourth Crusade and the Just War Theory', *Catholic Historical Review* 61 (1975). Secondly, there are studies which view the crusades against a wider theological background. The seminal work was C. Erdmann, *The Origin of the Idea of the Crusade* (see above), although many of Erdmann's views are now challenged (see especially J. Gilchrist, 'The Erdmann Thesis and the Canon Law, 1083–1141', in *Crusade and Settlement*, ed. P. W. Edbury, Cardiff, 1985). See also E. Delaruelle, *L'idée de croisade au moyen âge* (Turin, 1980); E. D. Hehl, *Kirche and Krieg im 12. Jahrhundert* (Stuttgart, 1980); J. S. C. Riley-Smith, 'Crusading as an Act of Love', *History* 65 (1980); B. Z. Kedar, *Crusade and Mission* (Princeton, 1984). For critics of crusading in the twelfth and thirteenth centuries, see E. Siberry, *Criticism of Crusading, 1095–1274* (Oxford, 1985).

A related subject is crusade preaching, for which see P. J. Cole, *The Preaching of the Crusades to the Holy Land, 1095–1270* (Cambridge, Mass., 1991); C. T. Maier, *Preaching the Crusades: Mendicant Friars and the Cross in the Thirteenth Century* (Cambridge, 1994) and *Crusade Propaganda and Ideology: Model Sermons for the Preaching of the Cross* (Cambridge, 2000). Yet another field of study, liturgy, is opening up and books on crusade masses, *clamores* and trentals by A. Linder, and on the liturgy of the Holy Sepulchre by C. Dondi, are eagerly awaited.

For studies of crusade literature (epics, songs and plays), see M. Böhmer, *Untersuchungen zur Mittelhochdeutschen Kreuzzugslyrik* (Rome, 1968); C. T. J. Dijkstra, *La chanson de croisade* (Amsterdam, 1995); P. Hölzle, *Die Kreuzzüge in der okzitanischen und deutschen Lyrik des 12. Jahrhunderts: das Gattungsproblem 'Kreuzlied' im historischen Kontext*, 2 vols (Göppingen, 1980); M. de Riquer, *Los Trovadores: Historia literaria y Textos*, 3 vols (Barcelona, 1983); S. N. Rosenberg and H. Tischler,

Chanter m'estuet: Songs of the Trouvères (London and Boston, 1981); D. A. Trotter, *Medieval French Literature and the Crusades (1100–1300)* (Geneva, 1988); F.-W. Wentzlaff-Eggebert, *Kreuzzugsdichtung des Mittelalters: Studien zu ihrer geschichtlichen und dichterischen Wirklichkeit* (Berlin, 1960).

R. C. Smail's magisterial study, *Crusading Warfare, 1097–1193* (Cambridge, 1956) has now a sequel in C. Marshall, *Warfare in the Latin East, 1192–1291* (Cambridge, 1992). J. France, *Victory in the East* (Cambridge, 1994) is dedicated to the military history of the First Crusade. See also the same author's *Western Warfare in the Age of the Crusades, 1000–1300* (London, 1999); R. Rogers, *Latin Siege Warfare in the Twelfth Century* (Oxford, 1992); J. Pryor, *Geography, Technology and War* (Cambridge, 1988); Y. Friedman, *Encounter between Enemies: Captivity and Ransom in the Latin Kingdom of Jerusalem* (Leiden, 2002); and D. Nicolle, *Arms and Armour of the Crusading Era, 1050–1350*, 2 vols (London, 1999).

The crusade was an instrument of the Papal Monarchy. Useful studies are A. Becker, *Papst Urban II (1088–1099)*, 2 vols (Stuttgart, 1964–88); H. Roscher, *Papst Innocenz III und die Kreuzzüge* (Göttingen, 1969); M. Maccarone, 'Studi su Innocenzo III. Orvieto e la predicazione della crociata', *Italia sacra* 17 (1972); C. R. Cheney, *Pope Innocent III and England* (Stuttgart, 1976); L. Thier, *Kreuzzugsbemühungen unter Papst Clemens V, 1305–1314* (Düsseldorf, 1973). See also S. Schein, *Fideles Crucis: The Papacy, the West and the Recovery of the Holy Land, 1274–1314* (Oxford, 1991); S. Menache, *Clement V* (Cambridge, 1998); and N. J. Housley, *The Avignon Papacy and the Crusades* (referred to above). For the financing of the crusades and developments in papal taxation, see especially W. E. Lunt, *Papal Revenues in the Middle Ages*, 2 vols (New York, 1934) and *Financial Relations of the Papacy with England*, 2 vols (Cambridge, Mass., 1939–62); and P. Guidi (ed.), 'Rationes decimarum Italiae nei secoli XIII e XIV. Tuscia. I. La Decima degli anni 1274–80', *Studi e Testi* 58 (1932).

Contributions to the study of individual crusades to the East are: R. J. Lilie, *Byzantium and the Crusader States, 1096–1204* (Oxford, 1994); M. Bull, *Knightly Piety and the Lay Response to the First Crusade: The Limousin and Gascony, c.970 – c.1130* (Oxford, 1993); G. Constable, 'The Financing of the Crusades in the Twelfth Century', *Outremer*, ed. B. Z. Kedar, H. E. Mayer and R. C. Smail (Jerusalem, 1982) and 'Medieval Charters as a Source for the History of the Crusades', *Crusade and Settlement*, ed. P. W. Edbury; R. Somerville, *The Councils of Urban II*, vol. 1: *Decreta Claromontensia (Annuarium Historiae Conciliorum*, Supplementum I (1972)); J. S. C. Riley-Smith, *The First Crusade and the Idea of Crusading* (London, 1986) and *The First Crusaders* (Cambridge, 1997); R. Chazan, *European Jewry and the First Crusade* (Berkeley, 1987) and *God, Humanity and History: The Hebrew First Crusade Narratives* (Berkeley, 2000); J. Prawer, 'The Jerusalem the Crusaders Captured: a Contribution to the Medieval Topography of the City', in *Crusade and Settlement*, ed. P. W. Edbury; J. Phillips (ed.), *The First Crusade: Origins and Impact* (Manchester, 1997); J. Shepard, 'When Greek meets Greek: Alexius Comnenus and Bohemond in 1097–8', *Byzantine and Modern Greek Studies* 12 (1988) and 'Cross-purposes: Alexius Comnenus and the First Crusade', *The First Crusade*, ed. J. Phillips; G. Constable, 'The Second Crusade as seen by Contemporaries', *Traditio* 9 (1953); J. Phillips and M. Hoch (eds), *The Second Crusade: Scope and Consequences* (Manchester, 2001); D. E. Queller and T. F. Madden, *The Fourth Crusade: The Conquest of Constantinople* (2nd edn, Philadelphia, 1997); J. Longnon, *Les compagnons de Villehardouin* (Geneva, 1978); J. M. Powell, *Anatomy of a Crusade, 1213–1221* (Philadelphia, 1986); W. C. Jordan, *Louis IX and the Challenge of the Crusade* (Princeton, 1979); D. Weiss, *Art and Crusade in the Age of Saint Louis* (Cambridge, 1998); A. Leopold, *How to Recover the Holy Land: The Crusade Proposals of the Late Thirteenth and Early Fourteenth Centuries* (Aldershot, 2000).

For the attempt to reinstate Peter the Hermit as originator of the First Crusade, see E. O. Blake and C. Morris, 'A Hermit Goes to War: Peter and the Origins of the First Crusade', *Studies in Church History* 22 (1984) and J. Flori, *Pierre l'Ermite* (see above).

Two good books on England and the crusading movement are C. J. Tyerman, *England and the Crusades, 1095–1588* (Chicago, 1988) and S. Lloyd, *English Society and the Crusade, 1216–1307* (Oxford, 1988). See also M. Keen, 'Chaucer's Knight, the English Aristocracy and the Crusade', in *English Court Culture in the Middle Ages*, ed. V. J. Scattergood and J. W. Sherborne (London, 1983).

When considering other theatres of war, consult in addition to the general works: for the Spanish crusades, D. W. Lomax, *The Reconquest of Spain* (London, 1978); R. A. Fletcher, 'Reconquest and Crusade in Spain *c.*1050–1150', *Transactions of the Royal Historical Society*, 5th ser., 37 (1987); P. Linehan, *The Spanish Church and the Papacy in the Thirteenth Century* (Cambridge, 1971); R. I. Burns, *The Crusader Kingdom of Valencia*, 2 vols (Cambridge, Mass., 1967); for the Baltic crusades, H. Beumann, *Heidenmission und Kreuzzugsgedanke in der deutschen Ostpolitik des Mittelalters* (2nd edn, Darmstadt, 1973); E. Christiansen, *The Northern Crusades* (London, 1986); for a crusade against Mongols,

P. Jackson, 'The Crusade against the Mongols', *Journal of Ecclesiastical History* 43 (1991); for crusades against heretics and opponents of the Church, N. J. Housley, 'Crusades against Christians: their Origins and Early Development, *c.*1000–1216', in *Crusade and Settlement*, ed. P. W. Edbury; M. Roquebert, *L'Epopée Cathare*, 3 vols (Toulouse, 1970–86), which is the best treatment of the Albigensian Crusade; S. Lloyd, ' "Political Crusades" in England, *c.*1215–17 and *c.*1263–5', in *Crusade and Settlement*, ed. P. W. Edbury; N. J. Housley, *The Italian Crusades* (Oxford, 1982), which is the best study of the political crusades in Italy.

For *milites ad terminum*, see G. Ligato, 'Fra Ordine Cavallereschi e crociata: "milites ad terminum" e "confraternitates" armate', *Militia Christi e Crociata nei secoli XI–XIII* (Milan, 1992), pp. 645–97; and for confraternities, J. S. C. Riley-Smith, 'A Note on Confraternities in the Latin Kingdom of Jerusalem', *Bulletin of the Institute of Historical Research* 44 (1971).

For images of crusading in art, music and literature of the nineteenth and early twentieth centuries, see E. Siberry, *The New Crusaders* (Aldershot, 2000).

The starting-point for the history of the military orders before 1312 is H. Prutz, *Die geistlichen Ritterorden* (Berlin, 1908). A. J. Forey, *The Military Orders from the Twelfth to the Early Fourteenth Centuries* (Basingstoke, 1992) is a good general history to 1312. See also A. Demurger, *Chevaliers du Christ: Les ordres religieux-militaires au Moyen Âge* (Paris, 2002); L. García-Guijarro Ramos, *Papado, cruzadas y órdenes militares, siglos XI–XIII* (Madrid, 1995). For their later history, see the chapter by A. T. Luttrell in J. S. C. Riley-Smith (ed.), *The Oxford Illustrated History of the Crusades* (as above). See also A. T. Luttrell and L. Pressouyre (eds), *La Commanderie, institution des ordres militaires dans l'Occident médiéval* (Paris, 2002). Many interesting papers are to be found in the proceedings of international conferences held at St John's Gate, Clerkenwell, in 1992 and 1996: M. Barber (ed.), *The Military Orders: Fighting for the Faith and Caring for the Sick* (Aldershot, 1994); H. Nicholson (ed.), *The Military Orders, Vol. 2: Welfare and Warfare* (Aldershot, 1998). A third volume, of papers delivered in 2000, and edited by W. G. Zajac, is expected soon.

For individual orders, see for the Temple: M. Barber, *The New Knighthood: A History of the Order of the Temple* (Cambridge, 1994) and *The Trial of the Templars* (Cambridge, 1978); A. Demurger, *Vie et mort de l'ordre du Temple* (Paris, 1985); H. Nicholson, *The Knights Templar: A New History* (Stroud, 2001); M. L. Bulst-Thiele, *Sacrae Domus Militiae*

Templi Hierosolymitani Magistri (Göttingen, 1974); A. J. Forey, *The Templars in the Corona de Aragon* (London, 1973); S. Cerrini (ed.), *I Templari, la guerra e la santità* (Rimini, 2000).

For the Hospital: H. J. A. Sire, *The Knights of Malta* (New Haven, 1994); J. S. C. Riley-Smith, *Hospitallers* (London, 1999) and *The Knights of St John in Jerusalem and Cyprus, c.1050–1310* (London, 1967); H. Nicholson, *The Knights Hospitaller* (Woodbridge, 2001); M. Gervers, *The Hospitaller Cartulary in the British Library (Cotton MS Nero E VI)* (Toronto, 1981); A. T. Luttrell, 'The Earliest Hospitallers', *Montjoie: Studies in Crusade History in Honour of Hans Eberhard Mayer*, ed. B. Z. Kedar, J. S. C. Riley-Smith and R. Hiestand (Aldershot, 1997), 'The Hospitallers' Early Written Records', *The Crusades and their Sources: Essays Presented to Bernard Hamilton*, ed. J. France and W. G. Zajac (Aldershot, 1998), *The Hospitallers in Cyprus, Rhodes, Greece and the West (1291–1440)* (London, 1978), *Latin Greece, the Hospitallers and the Crusades, 1291–1400* (London, 1982), *The Hospitallers of Rhodes and their Mediterranean World* (Aldershot, 1992) and *The Hospitaller State on Rhodes and its Western Provinces, 1306–1462* (Aldershot, 1999); J. Sarnowsky, *Macht und Herrschaft im Johanniterorden des 15. Jahrhunderts* (Münster, 2001); N. Vatin, *L'Ordre de Saint-Jean-de-Jérusalem, l'Empire ottoman et la Méditerranée orientale entre le deux sièges de Rhodes (1480–1522)* (Paris, 1994); R. Cavaliero, *The Last of the Crusaders: The Knights of St John and Malta in the Eighteenth Century* (London, 1960); V. Mallia-Milanes, *Venice and Hospitaller Malta, 1530–1798: Aspects of a Relationship* (Malta, 1992) and (ed.) *Hospitaller Malta, 1530–1798* (Malta, 1993); A. Hoppen, *The Fortification of Malta by the Order of St John, 1530–1798* (Edinburgh, 1979).

For the German orders: M. Tumler and U. Arnold, *Der Deutsche Orden vom seinem Ursprung bis zur Gegenwart* (5th edn, Bad Münstereifel, 1992); U. Arnold (ed.), *800 Jahre Deutscher Orden* (Gütersloh, 1990); M.-L. Favreau, *Studien zur Frühgeschichte des Deutschen Ordens* (Stuttgart, 1974); M. Tumler, *Der Deutsche Orden im Werden, Wachsen und Wirken bis 1400* (Vienna, 1955); W. Paravicini, *Die Preussenreise des Europäischen Adels*, 2 vols (Sigmaringen, 1989–95); M. Burleigh, *Prussian Society and the German Order* (Cambridge, 1984); F. Benninghoven, *Der Orden der Schwertbrüder* (Cologne, 1965).

For the Spanish orders: A. J. Forey, 'The Military Orders and the Spanish Reconquest in the Twelfth and Thirteenth Centuries', *Traditio* 40 (1984); D. W. Lomax, *La Orden de Santiago, 1170–1275* (Madrid, 1965): J. F. O'Callaghan, *The Spanish Military Order of Calatrava and its Affiliates* (London, 1975); L. P. Wright, 'The Military

Orders in Sixteenth- and Seventeenth-Century Spanish Society',
Past and Present 43 (1969).

For an English order: A. J. Forey, 'The Military Order of St
Thomas of Acre', *English Historical Review* 92 (1977).

On Islamic history, works of especial interest are: C. Hillenbrand,
The Crusades: Islamic Perspectives (Edinburgh, 1999); P. M. Holt, *The Age
of the Crusades: The Near East from the Eleventh Century to 1517* (London,
1986); C. Cahen, *Pre-Ottoman Turkey* (London, 1968); E. Sivan,
L'Islam et la croisade (Paris, 1968); M. Brett, 'The Near East on the
Eve of the Crusades', *La Primera Cruzada Novecientos Años Después*, ed.
L.García-Guijarro Ramos (Madrid, 1997); M. A. Köhler, *Allianzen
und Verträge zwischen fränkischen und islamischen Herrschern im Vorderen
Orient* (Berlin, 1991); M. G. S. Hodgson, *The Order of the Assassins*
(The Hague, 1955); R. S. Humphreys, *From Saladin to the Mongols: The
Ayyubids of Damascus 1193–1260* (Albany, 1977); R. Irwin, *The Middle
East in the Middle Ages: The Early Mamluk Sultanate, 1250–1382*
(London, 1986); D. O. Morgan, *The Mongols* (Oxford, 1986); H.
Inalcik, *The Ottoman Empire* (New York, 1973). There have been
some good biographies of sultans, in particular N. Elisséeff, *Nur ad-
Din*, 3 vols (Damascus, 1967); M. C. Lyons and D. E. P. Jackson,
Saladin (Cambridge, 1982); H. L. Gottschalk, *Al-Malik al-Kamil von
Egypten und seine Zeit* (Wiesbaden, 1958) and P. Thorav, *The Lion of
Egypt: Sultan Baybars I and the Near East in the Thirteenth Century* (London,
1987).

Index

The following abbreviations are used:

A	Abbot (of)	E	Emperor
Archbp	Archbishop (of)	K	King (of)
B	Bishop (of)	p. leg.	Papal Legate
C	Count (of)	Q	Queen (of)

Index

Index

Nicopolis, Crusade of, 82, 97
Nîmes, 13
Nogent-le-Rotrou, abbey of, 8
non-combatants, 37–8, 45–6, 69
Normandy, 50
Normans in S. Italy, 21, 65
Norway, 40, 96
Norwich, Bishop of, 97
Novit, 34

Octavian, Cardinal-B Ostia, p. leg., 44
Ösel, 93
Oliver, *scholasticus* of Cologne, 40
order-states, 84, 89
Orderic Vitalis, 62
Orvieto, 39
Otranto, 98
Otto of Grandson, 95
Ottobuono Fieschi, p. leg., 40–1
Ottomans, 16, 50, 69, 89,97–100

pacifism, 6–7
Palestine *see* Holy Land
palm fronds, 7–8
papacy, 3–5, 11, 22–3, 25, 27–37, 39, 45–8, 52,
    58, 62–3, 66–8, 70, 79, 81, 83–4, 87–8,
    92, 97, 104
  control of crusades, 31–5, 50–2, 87
Papal Monarchy, theory of, 31–5, 50, 104
Paris, 77
Paschal II, Pope, 16
peace in West, desirability of, 22, 35–7
peace movement, 36, 67
Pelagius, Cardinal-B Albano, p. leg., 51
penance, 3, 7, 54–5, 57, 60–4, 83
penitential violence, xii, 55–7, 83, 88
perpetual crusade, 30, 94
Peter I, K Cyprus, 81, 97
Peter III, K Aragon, 22
Peter Capuano, p. leg., 52
Peter of Blois, 62
Peter of Castelnau, p. leg., 19, 93
Peter of Sergines, Archbp Tyre, 78
Peter the Hermit, 28, 38, 41, 105
Peter the Venerable, A Cluny, 20
Peter Thomas, p. leg., 51
Philip, C Flanders, 92
Philip II (Augustus), K France, 19, 36, 44, 70
Philip II, K Spain, 99
Piacenza, 12–13, 27; *see also* councils of church
Piedmont, 96
pilgrimages, pilgrims, 2, 7–8, 34, 54–5, 57–8, 67,
    73, 83, 87–9
  peregrinatio religiosa, 54–5
Pisa, 21, 70
Pius II, Pope, 98
pledges, 44, 67–8

Poitiers, 13
Poland, 87, 96
Pont-Echanfray, family, 74
Post miserabile, 31, 36, 63–4, 93
preaching, xii, 5, 13, 17–18, 22, 28, 33, 35,
    37–43, 48, 52, 57, 61, 64–5, 103
  form of sermons, 42–3
  invitatio, 42
  use of songs, 42
priests *see* clerics on crusade; legates
privileges, 3, 31, 54, 66–8, 79, 87–9; *see also*
    essoin; protection
processions, 58–9
protection, 3, 5, 67–8, 87–9
Prussia, 30, 80–2, 84, 94–6

Quantum praedecessores, 15, 29–31, 63, 68, 92
Quia major, 31, 46, 93

Radulf, cistercian preacher, 38
Ralph Niger, 38
Ratisbon, Bishop of, 40
Raymond of St Gilles, C. Toulouse, 44
recruitment *see* response
redemption *see* vows
reform of Church, 14, 21, 32, 36, 73
relics, 22, 66
remission of sins *see* indulgences
response, 35, 48, 52, 72–3
return, 76
Rheims, Archbishops of, 59
Rhineland, 38, 71, 92
Rhodes, 81, 84–5, 95–6, 99
Richard, Earl of Cornwall, 94
Richard I, K England, 70, 77, 92
right intention (*intentio recta*), 6, 8, 48–9, 53–85
    passim
Robert of Cléry (Clari), 19
Robert of Courçon, p. leg., 46
Robert the Monk, 10
Robert II, Duke of Normandy, 44
Robert of Roches-Corbon, 75–6
Roman Empire, 9, 11, 16, 31–2
Rome, 22, 32, 48, 61
Rotrou of Perche, C Mortagne, 8
Russia, 80–1, 87, 96
Rutebeuf, 79–80

St Gilles, 13
St Jacques-de-Provins, Abbot of, 78
St John of Jerusalem, Order of, 40, 47, 83–5,
    89, 91, 95–6, 99, 107
St Lazarus, Order of, 83
St Mary of the Germans, Order of, 29–30, 81,
    83–5, 93–4, 96, 107
  Reysen of, 81
St Thomas, Order of, 83, 108

113